Migrant Labor and Border Securities in Pop Culture

Migrant Labor and Border Securities in Pop Culture explores the conditions for migrant domestic, agricultural, and factory workers as that of continual crisis and examines how the borderlands are a workshop of neoliberalism. These borderland stories present a future of integrated networks in which the border is not just physical but temporal, separating the present time of crisis and migrant phobia, and a future of transborder interaction and settlement based on bridges and networks rather than walls and the proliferation of security technologies. Written in accessible prose for undergraduate and graduate students across American studies, immigration studies, media and cultural studies and more, this book examines the collective action seen in Latina/o cultural productions after the economic crisis and how they reach across racial and geographic lines to imagine new entities.

Camilla Fojas teaches American Studies and Media Studies at the University of Virginia. Her books include *Border Bandits: Hollywood on the Southern Frontier* (University of Texas Press, 2008), *Islands of Empire: Pop Culture and U.S. Power* (University of Texas Press, 2014), and *Zombies, Migrants, and Queers: Race and Crisis Capitalism in Pop Culture* (University of Illinois, 2017).

T0383710

Routledge Focus on Latina/o Popular Culture

The Routledge Focus on Latina/o Popular Culture book series provides readers with a succinct overview of critical topics spanning across Latina/o studies and pop culture. Each book narrows in on important cultural moments in Latina/o history and media, serving as a short, detailed introduction to pressing issues intersecting Latina/o and pop culture today.

Migrant Labor and Border Securities in Pop Culture
Camilla Fojas

Migrant Labor and Border Securities in Pop Culture

Camilla Fojas

Routledge
Taylor & Francis Group

LONDON AND NEW YORK

First published 2017 by Routledge

2 Park Square, Milton Park, Abingdon, Oxfordshire OX14 4RN
52 Vanderbilt Avenue, New York, NY 10017

Routledge is an imprint of the Taylor & Francis Group, an informa business

First issued in paperback 2019

Copyright © 2017 Taylor & Francis

Library of Congress Cataloging-in-Publication Data
Names: Fojas, Camilla, 1971– author.
Title: Migrant labor and border securities in pop culture /
    Camilla Fojas.
Description: New York, NY : Routledge, 2017. | Series: Routledge
    focus on Latina/o popular culture
Identifiers: LCCN 2017014243 | ISBN 9781138092181 (hardback)
Subjects: LCSH: Foreign workers, Latin American—United States. |
    Latin Americans—United States. | Border security—United
    States. | Mexican-American Border Region. | Immigrants in
    mass media. | Hispanic Americans in mass media.
Classification: LCC HD8081.H7 F65 2017 | DDC 331.5/
    440973—dc23
LC record available at https://lccn.loc.gov/2017014243

ISBN: 978-1-138-09218-1 (hbk)
ISBN: 978-0-367-89067-4 (pbk)

Typeset in Times New Roman
by Apex CoVantage, LLC

Contents

Introduction
Border Securities, Migrant Labor, and Crisis Capitalism

> Precarization is not an exception, it is rather the rule. It is spreading even in those areas that were long considered secure. It has become an instrument of governing and, at the same time, a basis for capitalist accumulation that serves social regulation and control.
>
> —Isabell Lorey, *State of Insecurity*

Capitalism runs on crisis. Its boom and bust phases are deemed a natural lifecycle of life, death, and rebirth in an endless sequence. The organic cycle attributed to capitalism makes its mood swings seem unassailable rather than the mutable consequence of planning. Crisis provides the alibi for austerity measures that change the very shape and functioning of capitalist institutions, ultimately making them more flexible and adaptable and thus more profitable. And crisis spurs the production of knowledge. Marxist economist Richard D. Wolff reminds us that the economic crisis of 1848 provoked Marx's insights about the dynamics of capitalism. He argues that the Great Recession renewed interest in Marxism.[1] Yet if the recurrence of Marxism shifts according to capitalist boom and bust cycles, then social critique likewise follows the vicissitudes of provocation and oblivion. Crisis requires, at least in the short term, forgetting. It demands forward movement, expedient action, and absorption in the present. Marx provides lessons on how to transform the ruin of economic devastation into a rallying cry for social change by reckoning with the inciting events of crisis. And, forestalling oblivion, he links these crises diachronically to deepen potential critique and initiate social transformation.

There are episodic crises that achieve spectacular dimensions by virtue of their scale and subsequent global impact. The economic crisis of 2008 seemed to augur the demise of capitalism in the freefall of global financial markets. For left cultural critics the end of the financial system is not a source of anxiety or fear but of possibility, of an open future of new social movements and the potential for wholesale transformation of the economic order. The global crisis of 2008 was not the end of capitalism; it was not even the end of capitalism as we know it. Yet, the mood of crisis impacted cultural productions, created new stories, new connections across time and place, new ways of thinking about those in the quicksand of economic insolvency. For the precariat, precarious proletariat, crisis is persistent and intransigent, and this condition is nowhere more apparent than in the U.S.-Mexico borderlands. Many of the border stories that circulate in this moment share an intensity of political expediency and recognize the need for major social transformation. For example, Cesar Chavez reemerges across the pop cultural landscape in 2014 because the movements of the 1960s and 1970s demand reckoning and are ever more relevant post-crisis.

Much of recent cross-border Latino cultural productions address the social conditions of inequity besetting those at the bottom of the labor market, those first sacrificed in an economic crisis, immigrants and migrants who work and live at or near the border or in the margins as domestic, sweatshop, factory, or agricultural labor; some examples are the documentaries *Maquilapolis* (2006) and *Made in L.A.* (2007), feature films *Sleep Dealer* (2008), *Los Bastardos* (2008), *Machete* (2010), and *Cesar Chavez* (2014), and novels *Lunar Braceros 2125–2145* and *Barbarian Nurseries*. And these are only a few examples from the many productions that thematize the borderlands as a space of economic crisis and social activism. For instance, *Cesar Chavez* is a fairly conventional Hollywood narrative that targets a large mainstream audience to send a message about the struggles of migrant workers deprived of basic rights. It is a melodrama that, while focusing on the individual and his family, goes against some of the conventions of the genre to explore the political and cultural context of local and national labor organizing. *Maquilapolis* offers a documentary counterpoint to the ways that major Hollywood studios depict Latinas. It shows the steps and stages of women engaging in collective action as agents and subjects of the story. And it shows women in active roles without framing them in a sexualized manner. Though *Maquilapolis* may not have received the wide distribution and theatrical release of *Cesar Chavez* and *Machete*, it was shown nationally on the PBS "Point of View" (POV) series and continues to be screened in various venues.

Maquilapolis (2006) was released just as the U.S. economy was showing signs of economic distress and takes place following the economic downturn of 2001; it focuses on the border industrialization program and its outcomes along the Mexican side of the border. Like one of its border media precursors, Mexican-Chicano coproduction *Raíces de sangre*, this cross-border documentary thematizes the struggle of women working in *maquiladoras*, but it uses an experimental approach to their stories, allowing each woman to control the means of production of her own story within an overarching narrative of political organization against worker rights violations—it does what *Cesar Chavez* purports to do, which is to allow the poor to narrate their histories and control their futures. The future of the borderlands, in much speculative media, is not a better world. Alex Rivera's *Sleep Dealer* imagines the kind of technologized future world that demands "work without the workers," particularly if they are deemed undesirable migrants. And *Los Bastardos* is about such migrants. This independent film written and directed by Mexican cineaste Amat Escalante traveled the festival circuit in Mexico, Europe, and Latin America to much acclaim, and was an official selection in the Cannes film festival. In a verité style, it shows twenty-four hours in the life of Jesús and Fausto, two undocumented migrant day laborers in Los Angeles. The audience experiences their daily lives as they seek work, take long rides on the bus, and endure dehumanizing treatment everywhere they circulate.

Another timely documentary about migrant workers, *Made in L.A.*, examines the conditions for women in the L.A. garment industry. Like *Maquilapolis* it documents their struggles for fair wages and working conditions and offers a hopeful possible future for workers seeking to attain and secure their rights. In a fictional but no less activist approach, Robert Rodriguez's *Machete* makes day laborers the heroes in the revolutionary transformation of the social order. The film is about an ex-Federale masquerading as a day laborer in Austin, Texas. It uses the exploitation grindhouse genre to tell a different story about organizing and social change; rather than promulgating participation in a corrupt democratic process, the characters build a movement through coalition building and enact change through revolution. Each of these cultural productions engages different genres, often mixing or expanding the boundaries of genre to give a different take on the migrant condition along with different modes and methods for addressing their social and cultural status during times of economic crisis.

Migrant Labor and Border Securities in Pop Culture explores media that take place in some relation to the U.S.-Mexican border in the time leading up to and just following the 2008 economic crisis, or what critics have called the "fourth global crisis of the capitalist system."[2] Border media explore the depredations of capital, of a global economic order that requires racialized bodies performing irksome labor to sustain it. Perhaps the most iconic emblems of migrant labor are the *bracero* and the *doméstica* as temporary and unsecured workers who are marginal to the nation and its metonymic family while sustaining and supporting these entities. These stories expose the vicissitudes of belonging for the migrant while they also point to the conditions of workers post-crisis who are likewise rendered obsolete or precarious or literally displaced from their homes. And, for the migrant, crisis is not episodic, not a consequence of economic downturns, but a condition of living in a bordered world. Thus what has been occurring for years along the border suddenly, post-2008, became part of mainstream discourse and popular culture. The borderlands economies already witnessed the ongoing degradation of conditions including the loss of jobs, lowering of wages, homelessness and declining housing conditions, ecological ruin, feminization and temp-ification of the workforce, economic migration, and loss or lowering of benefits.

The borderlands are symptomatic of the neoliberal restructuring of the economic order in which production migrates just below the border to evade taxes, pay low wages, and avoid environmental regulations. The border is not merely symbolic of capitalism at the end of the line, it is where economic, ecological, and personal crises are unrelenting effects of the expansion of neoliberalism. Border narratives expose the contradictions of capitalism. These cultural productions document crisis and collective action in response to it, adding them to the historical record and to social memory. They offer creative solutions for organizing, resisting, and countering the story of capitalism as cyclical and relentless and as an inevitable outcome of the natural world. In this way, border stories already contain a kernel of critique and carry incredible potential to foment alternate fictions that challenge capitalism.

Notes

1. Richard D. Wolff, *Capitalism's Crisis Deepens: Essays on the Global Economic Meltdown 2010–2014* (Chicago: Haymarket Books, 2016).
2. Sasha Lilley, *Capitalism and Its Discontents: Conversations With Radical Thinkers in a Time of Tumult* (Oakland: PM Press, 2011), 1.

1 Border Securities and Unsecure Labor

In *Day Without a Mexican* (2004), a character played by Yareli Arizmendi, also co-writer of the script, asks, "How do you make the invisible, visible?" The answer is apparent in the film's title. She refers to the invisibility of Mexicans apparent in their unseen labor during a time of increasing phobia about migrants. This sentiment coincides with the concerns about the importance of making visible and documenting the history of the marginalized during uncertain and insecure times. Jesús Salvador Treviño, Chicano activist and director, works against the tide of media that would render the story of Chicana and Chicano and migrant struggle into oblivion. In *Eyewitness: A Filmmaker's Memoir of the Chicano Movement*, he argues, using George Orwell's *1984* as a point of reference, that memory is linked to the "*collective* memory of society." And this memory is full of lapses, erasures, and falsifications.

While we may not have a malevolent Big Brother monitoring us and daily altering yesterday's fact, we do have omnipresent mass media that in many ways serve a similar function. The evening news, documentaries, primetime television, radio, movies, and other forms of popular culture establish the facts of record, set the tone and parameters for their acceptance, endorse what will be remembered as historically important, and sanction what is valid in society.

From time to time, these facts of record are passed on to posterity through remembrance ceremonies such as anniversaries, revivals, sequels, and rediscoveries of events and individuals. They soon become incontrovertible history. It is the collective voice of mass media that can manipulate and alter our history—at times into a semblance virtually unrecognizable by the individuals who experienced it. *History is as the media tell us it is.*[1]

Media is the site of political representation and contestation. For Treviño it is a critical archive of memory. He argues:

> If mass media ignore an event, it simply didn't happen. Although individuals may remember the importance of a given event, unless validated by the media, its significance for society may be forever lost in a black hole of cultural forgetfulness. Mexican Americans know this only too well.[2]

The historical record is dynamic and might be altered and revised to include untold stories. He documents the Chicano movement in his roles as filmmaker and as a witness of events that "never found their way into American history texts or the popular culture's understanding of this period."[3]

Treviño documents what the news media did not. Randy Ontiveros describes how, during the 1960s and 1970s, the major networks earned a reputation for "bold coverage of the black civil rights movement," yet rarely depicted the Chicano civil rights movement except in a dismissive manner. This "brown out" or media occlusion of *el movimiento* is apparent in the CBS evening news coverage of the Chicana and Chicano activists invading Catalina Island as part of their "March of the Reconquest" to highlight land ceded by the U.S. The news frames this event as the threat of siege by an internal alien that is readily neutralized. Thus the news storyline assuages viewer anxiety by framing government intervention as a sign of state protection and security of its citizenry. The political meaning of the event, the act of protest, is never broached, and the wider political and historical context is nowhere apparent. This is part of a broader approach by major news networks to marginalize and occlude the Chicano movement and only grant it moments of visibility as a deleterious force in the U.S. or as one that might be co-opted and neutralized.[4] For instance, though the news media covered Cesar Chavez widely, it was only within a limited binary accorded Chicano and Chicana activists as either a martyred and humble Mexican or bloodthirsty revolutionary. The media embraced Chavez as the former in a manner that persists.

Salvador Treviño worked for many years in Hollywood film and television and in independent productions to tell stories of those marginalized by mass media. His long list of accomplishments includes producing the monumental PBS series "Chicano! The History of the Mexican American Civil Rights Movement" and directing the groundbreaking series "Resurrection Boulevard." He also directed *Raíces de sangre*, the first Mexican and Chicano cinematic co-production to document the realities of the border region and of Mexican migrants for cross-border audiences. *Raíces de sangre* challenges the chauvinism of dominant media in both the United States and

Mexico about labor and migrants in the borderlands. The film was the consequence of former Mexican President Luis Alvarez Echevarría's attempt to restore confidence in the state for Mexicans at home and *afuera* by diminishing political censorship and repression, particularly in the media. He forged links in personal meetings with Chicano leaders like Cesar Chavez and organizations, giving publicity to the conditions of Chicanos during the 1960s and 1970s in the United States. One consequence of this democratic *apertura* was the disbursement of funding that resulted in the first Chicano film produced in Mexico featuring Chicano and Mexican actors and helmed by a Chicano director, Treviño. *Raíces de sangre* documents the struggle of Chicanos around immigrant rights and labor issues for migrant workers and those working along the border region in *maquiladoras*. It takes place during an era of what David Maciel describes as a "discovery" of the Chicano community as a political entity and a market for Mexican goods and media.[5] This film set the tone and raised the standard for border films and Chicano and Latino films; it draws on the history and context of transnational labor migration and political organizing while establishing the importance of linking worker struggles across the border into Mexico and beyond.

Almost forty years later, U.S. and Mexican production companies Televisa and Lionsgate join forces to produce a biopic, shot mostly in Mexico, of Chicano activist Cesar Chavez by Mexican actor and director Diego Luna and Mexican and Mexican American actors and actresses. Luna is part of a generation of Mexican cross-over or, more accurately, global talent— including Gael García Bernal (also a producer of *Cesar Chavez*), Guillermo del Toro, Alejandro González Iñárritu, Alfonso Cuarón, and Salma Hayek, among others. The film is nominally part of a slate of film and other media that targets labor policy and practices along the border during a time of heightened immigrant phobia and economic crisis, or what some cultural critics have called "the end times," a time when the economic system is no longer sustainable in its current form. And many of these cultural productions point to new collaborations and alliances across borders and across the migrant racial middle.

Cesar Chavez invokes the memory and history of *Raíces de sangre*. And the latter set the historical terms for many cross-border productions about migrant workers. In a key moment in *Raíces de sangre*, the organizers are planning a rally and protest but are barred from a public park by the city council. In an effort to circumvent the restriction on public gatherings, they propose that the event be transformed from a rally to a staged play in reference to Chicano theater as a space of activism. Theatrical productions and fictional narratives of which the film is a part and other fictional storylines are zones where audiences might recognize their common purpose and, as E.P. Thomson notes, "identify points of antagonistic interest" that might lead to recognition of their common struggle as a class.[6] The border zone is a place of many points of antagonistic interest, of crisis, of the inequities created by capitalism, and where migrant identity is gathered and formed. It is a space of shared commonality, imagined and real.

The films of this chapter explore the migrant imaginary of popular culture through diverse aesthetic and generic modes and storylines. *Cesar Chavez* rendered the migrant story visible to wide audiences in the phatic tones of Hollywood melodrama. In stark contrast, the Mexican feature film, *Los Bastardos* (2008), does not appeal to audiences. Rather it challenges viewers, making them uneasy through exposure to the violent dynamics between U.S. citizens and Mexican migrant labor. Splitting the difference, *Machete* partakes in both a Hollywood mainstream and borderlands independent film aesthetic to deliver a politically charged message in a lively action film genre format. The post-crisis border films that explore the status and experience of migrant labor expose and dramatize "points of antagonistic interest" to move and mobilize audiences. In the tradition of cross-border post-*movimiento* culture, *Cesar Chavez*, *Los Bastardos*, and *Machete* work different aesthetic angles, genres, and narrative forms to similar effect. They expose audiences to the experiences of unsecure labor while, at times, exploring forms of activism.

Migrant Melodrama

Randy Ontiveros notes the exception to the media "brown out" during the civil rights era in the coverage of Cesar Chavez and the California grape strike. Chavez fit into the precepts of mainstream media representation of political struggle to become, in Todd Gitlin's words, a "media-certified celebrity leader."[7] And Ontiveros describes Chavez as part of the dichotomy of news media activist representation, discussed earlier, as either "suffering saints" or "dangerous radicals."[8] Chavez used television to gain visibility for oppressed workers at the same time that he cast himself in the role of "humble Mexican" to forestall any association of him with Latin American revolutionaries and to make his political message palatable to a wider public. This representational template set the terms for a similar melodramatic tone in the Hollywood version of the story.

Cesar Chavez presents the farm worker's movement within a melodrama of family dynamics in which father and son tensions present a point of coincidence between the growers and those struggling against them. The overarching story aspires to universality through this plot point while it delivers another story about the enactment of social change. The film is attentive to the history and tendency of Latino cinema to address issues relevant to its target audience, in this case, the work of organizing and building coalitions to create social change. The labor of migrants is rendered visible for a wide audience, drawing on the tradition of Latino Cinema—most notably *Raíces de sangre* and *Alambrista* (1977)—and the Chicano movement that sought the social, cultural, and political empowerment for those of Mexican descent in the United States. The film is more in line with the funding and production lineage of "Hispanic Hollywood" of the 1990s—*La Bamba* (1987), *American Me* (1992), *My Family/Mi Familia* (1995)—a consequence of post-civil rights demands for more nuanced representations of Latinos and Latinas in their families and communities of origin. *Cesar Chavez* draws on these traditions while glossing them.

Marshall Ganz, a labor organizer who worked on the staff of the United Farm Workers for sixteen years, describes the portrayal of Cesar Chavez in the film as caricatured and often departing from historical events to the point that the "lessons the film teaches contradicts the real lessons of Chavez's work." The weaknesses he identifies are exactly that of melodrama, of reducing complex historical events to a struggle between good and bad—the workers and the growers—while foregrounding a storyline of individual pathos and struggle. The historical Chavez exhibited incredible skills at coalition building and creating relationships with diverse constituencies and individuals, while the filmic Chavez is engaged in an often lone struggle against opposing forces. Ganz writes;

> Cesar's core leadership gifts were relational. He had an ability to engage widely diverse individuals, organizations and institutions with distinct talents, perspectives and skills in a common effort. The film, however, depicts him as a loner: driving alone (when in reality he had given up driving), traveling alone (which he never did) and deciding alone (when his strength was in building a team that could respond quickly, creatively and proactively to the daily crises of a long and intense effort).[9]

The film glosses the Farm Worker's Movement's deep connections to the civil rights movement and to others struggling towards similar ends: Filipinos (represented to some degree), African-Americans, the labor movement, and the larger Chicano movement (see Image 1.1 on page 10).

This is partly a result of the institutional constraints of major studio funded productions. In this case, the filmmakers, director and producers were beholden to a number of constituents, not the least of which was the Chavez family who had veto power over the script and the studios that seek marketability, defined as content that will appeal to liberal democratic ideals without threatening to alienate a white mainstream audience. *Cesar*

Image 1.1 A Coalition of Filipinos and Latinos March in Solidarity in *Cesar Chavez*

Image 1.2 Chavez Ponders the Conditions of Farm Workers

Chavez meets these competing demands by lionizing its protagonist and locating the struggle for equal rights in the domain of U.S. liberalism as an individual struggle.

The story follows Cesar Chavez in his emergence to social consciousness as a young man aware of the struggle of workers and their degradation by a system that values profit over human dignity (see Image 1.2).

He devotes his life and work to raising migrant worker consciousness— "you can't oppress someone who is not afraid anymore"—and to creating social change within democratic legal process, leading to the creation of the first law allowing migrant workers to organize. The struggle of Cesar Chavez as the representative of a racialized group is rendered within the story of the U.S as an exceptional political entity, a beacon of civil rights for the rest of the world, formed against outside forces in a paradoxically global and nativist sense. The film portrays a targeted boycott of a single grape grower, Bogdanovich, who exemplifies and symbolizes all other growers. When Bogdanovich aligns with then-President Nixon to have his grapes distributed abroad, thus bypassing the U.S. boycott, the struggle against the growers turns global. This is a major turning point in the film. The farm worker struggle ceases to be that of a marginal constituency and becomes the very sign of U.S. American liberalism. This is conveyed significantly in the scene that evokes the symbolic power of the Boston Tea Party that signaled the revolutionary spirit of the U.S. against British imperialism. The film tacitly alludes to this historical event when British dock workers, in alliance with the U.S. Farm Worker movement, throw Bogdanovich grapes into the harbor rather than unload them. This moment allegorizes how the film itself signals the full integration of the Latino narrative in the U.S. historical and cultural storyline, co-opting it as a sign of the revolutionary spirit of the U.S. In this way, the farm worker struggle is framed as relevant and significant to U.S audiences, and the film moves the activist work of peoples of color into the mainstream, making it palatable and accessible and neutralizing some of its antiracist valence (see Image 1.3).

Cesar Chavez puts the farm worker's movement squarely into the social world of global audiences, integrating actual footage from the era, giving the movement unprecedented publicity while appealing to U.S. cultural values. It elides many of the historical realities of this struggle and is complicit with Hollywood success stories, offering a story of individual triumph in the face of impossible odds. But it is a timely story that reminds viewers of the struggle of the poor during times of crisis and it is one that brings Mexican filmmaking, artists and producers into alliance with their U.S. counterparts.

Image 1.3 Multigenerational Marchers in *Cesar Chavez*

While *Cesar Chavez* is limited and constrained by industrial and capitalist demands, it keeps the history of *el movimiento* active in the popular imagination. Though the story follows a classical Hollywood structure that coincides with capitalist ideologies, the message resounds at the end. The biopic ends with Chavez expressing his desire to "see the poor take a very direct part in shaping society and let them make the decisions [. . .] if the poor aren't involved change will never come." The activists and organizers in *Maquilapolis* and *Made in L.A.*—discussed in the next chapter—show how women have put this idea into practice.

Migrant Discontent

Most activist storylines share a similar narrative that follows from discontent, disruption of a norm, and collective struggle that ends with some degree of social transformation toward more just conditions. *Los Bastardos* (2008) explores the unrest of migrant discontent along a different arc of development. It focuses on the psychic impact of exclusion, denigration, and dehumanization and shows the kind of action that ensues from this experience. The film is about two Mexican day laborers, Fausto and Jesús, who seek work in the parking lot of Home Depot in Los Angeles. They are waiting, and will work in the meantime, for nightfall when they can accomplish a lucrative job as hitmen. *Los Bastardos* is slow and methodical, even meditative; evident in the nearly four minute opening shot of the protagonists approaching from afar and dwarfed by the empty viaduct that surrounds them. This scene reflects their condition of homeless wandering and their diminishment within the larger social context in which they circulate. For them, the frustration of displacement, inhumane treatment, homelessness, and poverty quietly intensify.

The director of *Los Bastardos*, Amat Escalante, works in the style of renowned Mexican director Carlos Reygadas, also the film's associate producer, known for creating expressionistic and vivid imagery that reflects the psychic interiority of characters—examples of his films include *Japón* (2002), *Silent Light* (2007), and *Post Tenebras Lux* (2012). Like Reygadas, Escalante uses untrained actors along with trained actors, long takes and minimal editing in an overall verité style. The slow build in the action allows us to experience the relentlessness of the protagonists' work, which heightens the daily violence they experience within their persistent marginalization. Fausto and Jesús circulate in the impoverished zones of the city and in public spaces: parks, parking lots, and empty lots. Their main mode of transportation is that of the bus in a city defined by car culture, and public transportation is the refuge of the working poor who, in the bus scenes of the film, are presented exclusively as people of color.

Los Bastardos is clearly in contradistinction to the style of Hollywood Latino films about immigration like *El Norte* (1983), *My Family/Mi Familia* (1995), *Spanglish* (2004), and *Under the Same Moon* (2007), all of which tend toward the melodramatic to elicit audience sympathy for the migrants' difficult plight and to honor the work and workers that support the economy. These are all morally unambiguous and simple storylines that represent marginalized histories that, through the politics of positive representation, contest negative images and ideas about migrant labor.

Los Bastardos dispenses with the politics of representation to present a vexing ambiguity in which none of the characters from either side of the border are redeemed. Instead, Fausto and Jesús accept a job to murder a woman they have never met, Karen, for reasons that are unclear but that seem related to her involvement in a drug economy. The two men break into Karen's suburban L.A. home where she has just had dinner with her sullen and unresponsive teenage son. She eases her frustration with a hidden stash of crack cocaine. This is what we understand to be her undoing, some unpaid drug debt for which Fausto and Jesús must reckon. What follows is bizarre and haunting. The two men begin to occupy the home fully, making her serve them dinner, share drugs, take a dip in the pool, watch TV, as they toy with her in fake domesticity. If they are there to perform a routine hit, they take their time and, as a result, lull the audience into complacency. *Los Bastardos* inculpates the viewers in its workings, making them complacent and thus complicit in the violence that occurs. Until the final scene, the story builds hope that Karen will be left unharmed. The audience is mollified by the long takes and the characters' shared sense of abjection. Karen is initially terrified, then, like the audience, resigned (see Image 1.4 on page 14).

There is a clear shift of attention for Jesús in particular and somewhat for Fausto, from their "job" to exploring and enjoying the comforts of the middle class home they have entered unlawfully—in an obvious allegory of the U.S. as feminized domestic space. Fausto and Jesús are divided in their rapport with the home. Jesús inhabits the home and settles in while Fausto participates but maintains his distance, often watching Jesús and Karen from the sidelines. The latter's objectivity and disengagement will save his life and yet subject him to ever more alienation. He survives and remains in the U.S. but continues work under oppressive conditions as an undocumented migrant worker.

Fausto recognizes that they do not belong in the home and tries to break Jesús out of his domestic fever dream. It is Fausto who suffers the clarity of perception and the outcomes of the experience of oppression, sadness and frustration. For instance, when a group of teens yell racial epithets punctuated with a violent gesture, Jesús restrains Fausto from a counterattack and

Image 1.4 Jesús in *Los Bastardos*

the latter is reduced to tears. He has the same reaction while he is in Karen's house watching the television show "Cops" with her. The show reminds him that he will only ever be the denigrated object of racist state surveillance. We watch them watching, and while his reaction is emotional, hers is stoic. Upon realization of his abjection, he completes the job they were hired to do.

The violence featured on shows like the one they watch, particularly "America's Most Wanted" and "Cops," is typically about home invasions or domestic disturbances, particularly the racialized male invasion of a white feminine domestic space. This has become a mediated form of social anxiety about the nation as a vulnerable space invaded by rapacious Mexican intruders. The violence of the hit registers as a form of social vengeance, but it is also a mournful commentary on the status and role of the migrant in the U.S. The film ends with the shooter, Fausto, not released from his drudgery or oppression but working in a field under the unrelenting heat of the sun. Violence begets violence.

Los Bastardos is about crisis and the disruption of complacency. While it does not reflect the economic crisis in any overt way, it explores the ongoing crisis of dispossession, marginalization and exclusion for migrants. In a telling scene, a man hires day laborers, including Fausto and Jesús, from their post outside Home Depot. They are offered eight dollars an hour which they negotiate up two dollars and are promised a return trip back to the pickup site. Their work, significantly, is to clear the ground and dig the foundation for a home that they, continuing in this line of work, will never have the means to occupy. As they toil under the hot sun, all six, with shovels and pick-axes, work in silent unison and their labors form a machine-like and hypnotic industrial sound—reminiscent of the women of *Maquilapolis* who silently rehearse their labors in unison in the desert of the maquila landscape in a similarly choreographed performance. When the boss returns, he refuses them a ride back to Home Depot, claiming contradictorily that he never made such a promise and that he changed his mind. As the workers grumble, the boss realizes that he is outnumbered and acquiesces. This is an instance of insurrection and non-politicized recognition of the power of coalition. This scene occurs without the explicit markings of political speech or action, but impacts the audience unconsciously, if not consciously, for suggesting the power of the collectivity.

The violence of the film is a kind of reckoning. Fausto and Jesús are immersed in a violent world in which day laborers are treated as beasts of burden and sexual objects and work under precarious conditions in which they are subject to the arbitrary will of employers. They are not the engineers of the violence in the story though they carry it out. The film ponders what it would mean to literally bring migrant labor home to invade and usurp it. This is timely given the economic context of the housing market crash that displaced many people, mostly middle class homeowners, from their homes. And many erroneously inculpated the precariat as "subprime" borrowers for their victimization by unscrupulous lenders. If we shift our perspective on the debt economy, it could be argued that the U.S. has incurred a debt in the form of underpayment of undocumented workers. And this underpayment enacts continued economic exile, dispossession, inadequate housing and homelessness—Jesús and Fausto work on and in homes but are themselves homeless. Their occupation of Karen's home is transitory and unwelcome like that of migrant labor in the U.S. The violence that signals the end of the story and of Karen's life is shocking and tragic; it does not lead to revolutionary ideas about social change but is a mournful reflection of the unchanging conditions of migrant labor.

Machete, perhaps citing *Los Bastardos*, gives another interpretive take on the day laborer as hired gun to very different narrative ends, tone, and message. Robert Rodriguez's parody of immigration phobia, the *Machete* franchise—*Machete*, *Machete Kills* (2013), *Machete Kills in Space* (in development)—brings revolutionary ideas about collective organizing and social change to a general audience through a mix of the grindhouse style of filmmaking and the B-grade *cine negro* style of border filmmaking. *Machete* was released during a time of anti-immigrant hysteria, particularly in Arizona, and it appeared just prior to the bicentennial celebrations of Mexican independence. Machete (Danny Trejo) represents the cross-border provenance of the film as an ex-Federale from Mexico who works as a day laborer in Texas. He is a migrant worker who is not a passive object of immigration policy or worker politics but an action hero. He is hired to assassinate a senator regarded as racist, Senator McClaughlin (see Image 1.5) (Robert De Niro), only to be "double-crossed and left for dead," and so he must avenge himself of his would-be killers and in doing so, participate in the cause of collective antiracist struggle in a massive *Wild Bunch* style shootout.

Machete appears to be a common day laborer trying his luck with other workers. Yet he is an ex-Federale who, like Jesús and Fausto, is hired to perform a hit, in this case on a senator. The assassination attempt is a set-up and part of a larger intrigue to make the senator into a hero and justify his "tough on immigration" stance. And border policies are part of drug cartel manipulation of the market. The senator and his cronies are in business with this cartel and stand to profit from restricted cross-border traffic. As the senator publicizes his anti-immigration message, a resistance movement is coalescing, calling itself the "network." The storyline is about the development of a new social movement across racial and class lines while using the rhetoric of the Chicano civil rights movement to advance its message.

Image 1.5 Senator McLaughlin in a News Briefing

For example, Jessica Alba, ICE agent turned activist, using an anti-imperial political refrain, tells a group of workers, "we didn't cross the border, the border crossed us!" Like *Cesar Chavez*, *Machete* garners a mainstream audience while the storyline encodes a critical discourse about U.S. immigration policy. The advertising copy for *Machete* locates the film squarely in the action genre directed at Hollywood audiences:

> Set up, double-crossed and left for dead, Machete (Trejo) is an ass-kicking ex-Federale who lays waste to anything that gets in his path. As he takes on hitmen, vigilantes and a ruthless drug cartel, bullets fly, blades clash and the body count rises. Any way you slice it, vengeance has a new name—Machete.

The film actually targets two distinct markets: mainstream Hollywood, through its major stars—Jessica Alba, Lindsay Lohan, Don Johnson, Steven Seagal, and Robert De Niro, and a critical Latino border genre and its stable of stars—Danny Trejo, Michelle Rodriguez, and Cheech Marin. This is evident in the different previews and movie trailers directed at these two distinct audiences. Danny Trejo narrates the trailer intended for Latino audiences "in a special Cinco de Mayo message" that clearly targets anti-immigrant hysteria; whereas the Hollywood trailer, narrated by Jessica Alba, conveys a story about an individual hero whose successful struggle against the odds will be rewarded with the affections of Alba's character.

The film in its dual distribution took on a life beyond its immediate narrative order and spurred public outrage about the racialized conflict portrayed in the story. Zachary Ingle, citing the various ways the public commented on the film on blogs, discussion boards and YouTube videos, found that the film elicited a range of responses about its racial plot. In particular, syndicated radio host Alex Jones describes Machete as a symbol of Latin American revolution and the story one of liberation theology, while other critics, like Stephen Holden, found the film to be unthreatening except for those on the extreme right.[10] While these diverse responses point to a divided reception of the film, *Machete* is a story with social impact, one that might motivate audiences to act to change their circumstances. As an action hero, Machete (Image 1.6 on page 18) provokes and excites, turning the ethos of revolution into cultural capital for Hollywood viewers.

Like *Cesar Chavez*, *Machete* combines a storyline about an individual male hero struggling against a corrupt system within the context of collective struggles. Yet the male hero is the focus of these stories in a manner that coincides with U.S. exceptionalism, or the idea that a single character or entity might act alone and outside the strictures of law in a manner that

Image 1.6 Machete Stands His Ground

ultimately benefits the public or greater good; in these cases, the ends justify the means in a way that captures the ethos of the U.S. revolutionary
spirit. Yet, at odds with this ideology of individualism as the cornerstone of
capitalism is the larger context of collective organizing of these individuals,
one that is more akin to socialist practice.

Cesar Chavez and *Machete* publicize collectivist ideas through a sleight
of hand in which a storyline appears to fit the Hollywood pattern, but ultimately sends a message about the creation of alternate publics, ones in
which networks and assemblages of people might act against the prevailing social order to change it. Yet, these stories fail in some ways to rei-
magine gender dynamics along more collectivist lines. Women's roles are
sometimes powerful, as in the case of Dolores Huerta in *Cesar Chavez* and
"She" or Luz and Sartana in *Machete*, but these women remain ancillary to
the real heroes, though Huerta was a powerful and iconic organizer in her
own right. In *Machete*, in keeping with the grindhouse style, women are
fetishized and their power emanates from sexually charged visual appeal.
All of the women are hyper-feminine and stylized while Machete, the main
hero, played by sexagenarian Danny Trejo, is a non-typical romantic lead.

Cesar Chavez and *Machete* cater to mainstream and masculinist desires
and demands, and in doing so are able to reach much wider audiences with

messages about equal rights and social equality—though women are often sacrificed to this masculinist ideology. These pop cultural productions work different angles of social critique and social change during an era of economic crisis. They contain stories about a racialized migrant working class of seasonal, temporary, and ultimately disposable workers. And these workers allegorize the condition of all workers in a troubled economy. The main characters Cesar Chavez and Machete and to an extent Jesús and Fausto contest the idea that precarity demands compliance, that individual preservation should take precedence over social solidarity. Instead, in keeping with the tenets of the revolutionary use of media that emerged during the civil rights era in the principles of New Latin American cinema, Chicano cultural productions, and Latino film, they dramatize the demand for human rights and equality, antiracist struggles, and the right for self-determination. And they show that the struggle to obtain these demands is successful, issuing hope and optimism for new generations of media activists. These border films represent a reconfigured cultural politics around social movements that create networks and alliances across social divisions, cultural divides, and the borders between nations.

Notes

1. Jesús Salvador Treviño, *Eyewitness: A Filmmaker's Memoir of the Chicano Movement* (Houston: Arte Público Press, 2001), xi–xii.
2. Ibid, xii.
3. Ibid, xiii.
4. Randy Ontiveros, "No Golden Age: Television News and the Chicano Civil Rights Movement." *The Race and Media Reader*. Ed. Gilbert B. Rodman (New York: Routledge, 2014), 55.
5. David Maciel, *El Norte: The U.S-Mexican Border in Contemporary Cinema* (San Diego: Institution for the Regional Studies of the Californias, 1990).
6. Sasha Lilley, *Capitalism and Its Discontents: Conversations With Radical Thinkers in a Time of Tumult* (Oakland: PM Press, 2011), 14.
7. Cited in Ontiveros, 60.
8. Ibid, 56.
9. Marshall Ganz, "Not the Cesar Chavez I Knew." *The Nation*, 1 April 2014, np.
10. Zachary Ingle, "The Border Crossed Us: *Machete* and the Latino Threat Narrative." *Critical Approaches to the Films of Robert Rodriguez*. Ed Frederick Aldama. (Austin: University of Texas Press, 2014), 159–160.

2 Migrant Domestics and Gendered Work in Crisis Capitalism

In "Devious Maids" (Lifetime, 2013–2016), Carmen Luna, maid and aspiring entertainer, tries to find a job as an actress and discovers, ironically, that the only roles available to her are for maids. In U.S. popular culture, the maid is a type inaugurated by African Americans and consolidated by Latina and Asian figures. It is not uncommon for shows or films based in Los Angeles or New York to have a family with a Latina maid or, more recently, a Filipina domestic—an enduring sign of economic disparities.[1] Women in care or domestic work constitute the largest female migrant group globally, and much of this care work is performed in the largest cities in the global North.[2] Grace Chang, writing in 2000, notes that Asian and Latina migrant labor in global capitalism is often marginal and invisible. They are treated as disposable, not worthy of attention, and thus remain disenfranchised, exploited and undervalued. Chang's work is prescient and of an era at the same time. That is, prior to the 2008 economic crisis, migrants and their labors were unseen and underrepresented in public discourse. But, during and after the crisis, migrants are excruciatingly visible as sources and subjects of all that ails the social order. And those at the bottom of the labor market are the first and most visible sacrifices in the economic freefall. By the 2016 reissue of Chang's writings about "disposable domestics," several activist writers and thinkers had contributed their reflections, in both preface and afterword, on the major cultural shifts that have changed the conditions and possibilities for migrant workers. Alicia Garza, founding organizer of Black Lives Matter, writing in the afterword, links the social movements of migrant workers to those of Black women in the U.S., noting their common condition of criminalization and disposability.

> While there are vast, complex, and important differences between slavery and the exploitation and abuse of immigrants, there is something familiar about the legacy of a nation built on white nationalism and structural racism that, at the same time that it fights for the liberty of

its white and American propertied citizens, limits, makes conditional, or eliminates the freedom of those who built and continue to build the wealth on which this country survives.[3]

Garza notes that the criminalization of migrants along with mass deportations and detentions dovetails with the mass incarceration of African Americans as components of the same strategy of surveillance of peoples of color. And the structural inequities and subsequent forms of violence noted by Chang and Garza intensify with each downward economic shift. They call for greater alliances across laboring groups and organizations born of the recognition of their common predicament under global capitalism.

The cultural conditions following the economic crisis opened the way for greater visibility for those on the bottom of the labor market and for those who persist in conditions of servitude to the economically solvent. Domestic labor is popularized in the television show "Devious Maids" and through Hector Tobar's *Barbarian Nurseries* (published in 2011), and the emergence of a migrant and border worker movement comprised mostly of women can be traced in the documentaries *Maquilapolis* (2006) and *Made in L.A.* (2007). These texts critique the cultural and economic conditions besetting Latina workers. And each offers their version of alternate possible futures for oppressed labor. In particular, the documentaries express a vital political expediency different in tone from their predecessors in which the struggles for worker and immigrant rights are ever more pressing leading up to and following the economic freefall of the leading world economy that began in 2006 and that ended, for some, a few years later. They offer a range of remedies and imagined outcomes drawn from cross-border cultural productions across a number of different genres. These media powerfully contest working conditions and promulgate the assertion of workers' rights, particularly the right to association and to collective bargaining. And this activism is performed across racial, ethnic, and class lines. While activist oriented, they also reflect on the existential condition of living in crisis capitalism. There are moments in almost all of these productions in which the fundamental contradictions of capitalism are exposed as completely untenable.

Maid for TV Crisis

Veteran actress Lupe Ontiveros describes playing a maid more than 150 times during her long career. And the Latina maid is a staple in popular cultural productions. There are too many shows and films to mention, but some notable examples of productions featuring Latina domestics are "Will and Grace," "Family Guy," "Arrested Development," "Weeds," and *Maid in Manhattan* (2002) or *Spanglish* (2004). "Devious Maids" tackles this trope head on with humor and cynicism. This melodramatic show bordering on camp is based around the lives of five Latina maids in Los Angeles, the center of the soft power of the U.S., with Hollywood as a major fulcrum of capitalist storyforms. And the maid is the central character in Héctor Tobar's novel set in post-economic crisis Los Angeles, *The Barbarian Nurseries*. In "Devious Maids" and *The Barbarian Nurseries*, the maid plays against type, she shores up and exposes the ridiculousness of her elite bosses, their extravagance and waste, and she is the moral point of reference in the story. Both texts take place during the Great Recession and partake in a general public disregard for the economic elite represented by the bosses. The Latina maid in popular culture defines the role and function of migrant labor from the global South in the public imagination as a sign of economic inequality and racial capitalism, illustrating how capital relations are fundamentally racialized and unequal.

These popular cultural narratives perform several kinds of work. They convey the mythos, fantasies, and storyform of capitalism in scenarios of wealth and luxury while they expose the fundamental and irresolvable contradictions of the economic system. The migrant subplot suggests an alternate story to the mythos of uplift and capitalist revitalization, one that disrupts and defies capitalism's master narrative and lays the groundwork for a new fiction, a different possible future for the precariat, those at the very bottom of the global labor market. Taken together, they might provide clues about how to imagine new forms of solidarity. Like their labor organizing and student activist counterparts in California, the Filipinos and Latinos, mostly of Mexican origin, worked together for social justice—as in the film *Walkout*, about student protests led by a mestiza Filipina, and in *Cesar Chavez*, which alludes to Filipinos in the United Farm Worker struggles—though Filipinos had a much larger founding role in the history of the UFW. Only a few of these stories convey this possible alliance. And some do so obliquely, as in *The Barbarian Nurseries*, where the maid Araceli wears a "Filipina," a maid's uniform that is actually a Barong Tagalog, or a typically elegant shirt that originates in the Philippines. She is the only one of the maids in her neighborhood that wears one as a holdover from the customs of domestic service in her native Mexico City. This unique mixing of Mexican and Filipino culture is the result of the Manila-Acapulco galleon trade that created a cultural exchange that brought the "Filipina," mangoes and other things to Mexico and brought Mexican cuisine, words, and flora to the Philippines. This shirt, the "Filipina," is also called the *guayabera*, and is common in Cuba and parts of Latin America and Central America. These narratives about Mexican and Filipina domestics suggest continuities, possible alliances across the "racial middle" comprised of Asians and Latinos from the point of view of those at the bottom of the labor market in crisis capitalism. The alliances across borders and racial and laboring groups are much more explicitly drawn in documentaries, particularly *Maquilapolis* and *Made in L.A.*: the latter is about seamstresses in sweatshops in L.A., equally gendered work that employs only or mostly women. These texts explore the current conditions of global indentured servitude across racial and national borders, and they offer remedies for the condition of alienation and subjugation.

The Barbarian Nurseries is about the cultural landscape of an L.A. divided and reflected in the Torres-Thompson household, helmed by mixed-race Scott and Anglo Maureen. This is not about the city as the seat of Hollywood but one impacted by the economic crisis that began in 2007. The family is over-leveraged, particularly after huge losses in the stock market, and must get rid of their gardener and nanny, but retain their maid, Araceli, who, like most workers after the Great Recession, takes on more work for the same wages, in this case of both nanny and maid. The crux of the plot turns on a "misunderstanding" that occasions multiple misapprehensions that ultimately land Araceli in jail. A fight about Maureen's overspending turns violent when Scott pushes her and she falls backwards, unhurt but shaken. Each separately decides to take a couple of days away without informing the other. Two days becomes three and Araceli, left with the children, becomes increasingly desperate, eventually deciding to venture out in search of the children's grandfather, armed only with a photograph with an L.A. address from decades ago. The children are declared missing and kidnapped and she is wrongly charged with child endangerment, both Maureen and Scott's fault for spreading misinformation to protect themselves. A media circus ensues in which all manner of pundits and activists, both left and right, voice their claims around the issue of immigration and undocumented labor. The ideological rifts between and diverse realities of the white mainstream and the Latino communities become apparent. Araceli predicts the conditions of this changed economic and racial order: "She wondered if she was living at the beginning of a new era, when the pale and protected began to live among the dark and sorrowful, the angry multitudes of the south."[4] Such is the case after this fiasco; Scott and Maureen decide to live without a maid, move to a smaller house and put their kids in public schools. Araceli is freed and sets out with her Mexican American boyfriend to an uncertain future, but one of her own making, as they journey to Arizona and perhaps to Mexico.

An almost too-perfect counterpoint to these examples is the Lifetime series, produced by ABC studios, "Devious Maids," which engages a range of Latino popular cultural producers, including executive producer Eva Longoria, and is the first prime time show to feature an all Latina cast: Puerto

Rican actress Roselyn Sanchez, known for her role in *Rush Hour 2*, Ana Ortiz of "Ugly Betty," Judy Reyes from "Scrubs," Dania Ramirez, and Edy Ganem (all pictured in Image 2.1).

One of the writers is well-known playwright Tanya Saracho who, with Coya Paz, founded in 2000 in Chicago *Teatro Luna*, a theater group dedicated to countering stereotypical images of Latinas in media. Other writers are Anahí López, who wrote for the Mexican telenovela from which "Devious Maids" is adapted, "Ellas son . . . la alegría del hogar," and Gloria Calzada, who wrote for the Colombian novela "Yo soy Betty, la fea." Whereas the other texts feature sullen and miserable migrants, "Devious Maids" is more in line with Hollywood film versions of the maid. Isabel Molina-Guzmán, in her discussion of *Spanglish* and *Maid in Manhattan*, explores how the maid is romanticized to defuse the threat she poses as an immigrant and potential site of terrorism; she becomes instead a consumable body that nurtures white domesticity.[5] But these maids are a slight revision of their Hollywood kin. They are not just romantic objects; they are also devious subjects. The show is about spectacles of affluence as the source of ambivalence, both moral outrage and attraction.

The show centers around several maids (pictured in Image 2.2 on page 26) and their bosses. It engages the fantasy of subversion, that the maids might work together to undermine and dismantle the structures of power that beset

Image 2.1 The All-Latina Ensemble Cast of "Devious Maids"

their own ambitions—they are, in their own words, "maids who solve murders." We, via the maids as proxies, are spies in this world, privy to the decadent and profligate machinations of the powerful. Yet, in keeping with the genre of melodrama, moral dilemmas and social contradictions are readily resolved with simple solutions. Irene Mata calls this "ideological containment" in which the immigrant story is kept simple with resolvable conflicts and clear moral worlds in service of a story of betterment and uplift.[6] Indeed, solutions on the show are simple and clear. Character in the way? Kill him! Need your papers? Marry your boss! The latter is a plotline from a sitcom of the 1980s called "I Married Dora" which reappears in "Devious Maids." Unlike *The Barbarian Nurseries*, the series does not broach the more difficult political issues related to undocumented labor migration. In *The Barbarian Nurseries*, as Araceli reviews the room of the young children in her care, she notes how the space expresses her own privations. She calls it the Room of a Thousand Wonders "because it was filled with objects designed to amaze and delight." The novel does different work from these media texts, because in it we are privy to her internal musings through close third-person narration: "Araceli felt self-pity and resentment at the absences and inequalities that were the core injustices of her existence." And we are privy to her internal thought: "*It is a big world, divided between rich and poor, just like those humorless lefties at the university said. What would I have become with a mother like Maureen and a room like this?*"[7] The reader understands her predicament within a broader, more nuanced social and political world.

The ideological gloss of "Devious Maids" signals its ultimately conservative narrative, one that coincides with that of the economic elite, based on the premise that the economic and social order, if disrupted, will be restored. And the show promotes the idea that fighting this order is misguided, deluded, and even a sign of madness. For instance, one of the subplots of "Devious Maids" is about a masked group of bandits—mostly sons of the maids—who act as robin hoods, and claim to be fighting "income inequality." They are revealed to be invidious and misguided youth with dark urges that disrupt the fun of the narrative, and they are quickly neutralized—to make this point clear, one of the episodes about them is called "Bad Seed."

Susan Lucci of "All My Children" fame is one of the bosses who treats Zoila, her maid, like "one of the family" or "like a sister." And within the imagination of the series, they are family. Zoila chooses Lucci's character over her own sister and their children are engaged to be married. In her groundbreaking work, *Maid in the USA*, Mary Romero finds that this kind of language obviates a discussion of the very conditions of labor under which maids work. She writes that "Housework is ascribed on the basis of gender, and it is further divided along class lines and, in most cases, by race and ethnicity. Domestic service accentuates the contradiction of race

Image 2.2 Organizing the Maids Over Lunch

and class in feminism, with privileged women of one class using the labor of another woman to escape aspects of sexism."[8] Domestic service raises challenges to the "feminist notion of 'sisterhood.'" And the idea that the maid is "one of the family" obviates discussions of the precariousness and vulnerability of this class of workers, their lack of legal protections, infantalization, and, ultimately, their disposability.

The precariousness of this work keeps racialized populations at the bottom of the labor market in competition rather than in coalition. "Devious Maids" refers to Asian-Latina competition without resolving it. There are a couple of occasions when an Asian maid is brought in to replace one of the devious maids, and they are pit against each other. Until Joy, played by Korean American actress and transracial adoptee Joy Osmanski, and Zoila align under the "maid code." But this storyline is quickly dispensed. Grace Chang writes of how Asian and Latina workers, by virtue of their transnational ties, share the same status as "disposable domestics." She notes, with others like Pamela Sparr, that structural adjustment programs rendered by the IMF and World Bank caused the conditions—resource depletion, debt, and poverty—for migration to the global North, where, without aid, they are forced into the bottom of the labor market where they remain. These conditions, shared by the maids across racial and ethnic divisions, are obscured by storylines about their separation and competition with each other, but even these stories offer clues about a possible future of alliance and cooperation. Yet, as "Devious Maids" shows, too much optimism represses conflict and discontent. It obviates the potential of revolutionary critique, whereas misery—Tobar's "miserable migrant"—opens an abyss, an aporia, from which real social transformation might emerge. Revolutionary critique refuses remedy, easy solutions, hope and deferral to some sunnier future. It is the pessimism of the sad order of things in their current state and the demand for another possible future, another story, or a new fiction.

These stories take place in the context of crisis, not simply the economic crisis but the neoliberal crisis of austerity as well as the race to the bottom in wages that create precariousness and worker compliance. As workers work harder and put in longer hours to retain their positions, leisure time becomes an ever-diminishing commodity. The latter is the most important condition for action and theorizing social transformation. Melissa Wright argues that women are oppressed and dehumanized in the very modes of production into which they are enmeshed. Within feminized work, women are deemed disposable in a manner drawn from the patriarchal constitution of domestic space that puts women in subordinate positions within the household. Women are subject to the patriarchal order within production that forms a continuum with domestic labor. Women's work is ancillary and devalued, and those who perform it are likewise undervalued and disposable. She explores this idea in the context of factory work and in the media representation of activists fighting against conditions that enable femicides in Ciudad Juárez along the border. She reminds us that Marx defines profit as unremunerated labor so that those who profit from it are "stealing resources from workers."[9]

Made to Mobilize

Maquilapolis is the result of independent and collective binational efforts by Vicky Funari and Sergio De La Torre in collaboration with the women of Grupo Factor X, Chilpancingo Collective for Environmental Justice, and Women's Rights Advocates, co-produced by the Independent Television Service and partially funded by the Sundance Institute Documentary Fund. The film approaches worker struggle on the border with little regard for marketability or profit-seeking. It is the result of the collaboration between U.S.-based filmmakers and the Mexican women who commandeer the camera to tell their own stories and enact their own struggles against major corporations along the border. The documentary has a stated aim expressed by the filmmakers as a cross-border campaign for social change through mediamaking:

We are currently seeking funding to implement a binational Community Outreach Campaign, designed and implemented collaboratively with stakeholder organizations in the U.S. and Mexico. The campaign utilizes a high-profile public television broadcast, top-tier film festivals, and community screenings of the film to create meaningful social change around the issues of globalization, social and environmental justice and fair trade. Our outreach team includes dedicated activists on both sides of the border, media makers committed to social change, and most importantly a group of women factory workers struggling to bring about positive change in their world.[10]

This collaborative production and the political initiatives it documents and encourages enact the ideals of cross-border political organizing. The women at the bottom of the *maquiladora* labor market commandeer cameras to tell a story that involves their struggle against the factory owners. Their activist work is not mediated by either the filmmakers, in the case of the documentary, or the unions which, as *Raíces de sangre* also reveals, are under the employ of the owners, not the workers. They make the decisions about how they will organize and act and shape the direction of their own futures.

In *Maquilapolis* the women's stories are conveyed within a larger historical and social context that implicates economically driven policies of the United States, in particular, the Border Industrialization Program (BIP) and the North American Free Trade Agreement (NAFTA). The documentary explains how the Border Industrialization Program of 1965 initiated the creation of the *maquiladoras* or foreign-owned assembly plants in the "free trade zones" along the Mexican side of the U.S.-Mexico border and invited U.S. manufacturers to move their operations to this area. *Maquilapolis* describes waves of development that intensified and expanded after the passing of NAFTA and that deepened the exploitation of workers' rights. This is conveyed in images of the production and destruction of factory spaces to convey the economic cycles of capitalism. Once the border economy proves to be less than profitable, the factories move elsewhere. The film shows images of the vacant, ruined, and abandoned spaces to convey corporate disregard for local economies. The women visually document these spaces and narrate their hidden story; for instance, Carmen Durán explains how Sanyo closed shop and moved to Indonesia in search of lower wages. The corporation abandoned its factory space and its workers, to whom they refused to pay severance wages. Durán, along with several colleagues, initiates legal action against Sanyo to recuperate lost wages and eventually succeeds.

The documentary uses some experimental, non-narrative techniques to shape the mood and meaning of the images. The women's monotonous and rote work is conveyed not in factory scenes, but in images of nine workers dressed in blue factory uniforms dramatizing their repetitive labors like a choreographed installation in an abandoned lot. Their work is rendered a kind of dignified aesthetic experience, meditative and graceful. The music that accompanies this scene is composed of industrial sounds from or imitating the machines of the factories. While their work is dignified in this aesthetically appealing sequence, the narrative conveys the oppressive conditions of their work that includes risks to their health, lack of job security, and violation of their rights. Also, the shift work they perform is often out of conjunction with the daily schedules of their children, and many of them are without partners to share in the domestic work. They live in precarious circumstances in which the loss of employment or the diminishing of wages has devastating effects.

In addition to the struggle to work and maintain a household, these women are beset by rising toxicity in their environments, both in the factories and in the areas surrounding their homes. One of the women, Lourdes Luján, describes a river that runs through a neighborhood that turns various colors and emits noxious fumes when the factories dump waste into it under the cover of rain. She describes how, when she was a child, people in the neighborhood or *colonia* would swim and camp along its shores. Now such use of the river is unimaginable. Lourdes and Carmen Durán, her colleague, catch the river in full toxic bloom on camera as they jokingly mock-report on it like newscasters. This footage is a key visual indictment of environmental violations that solidifies their case against the *maquiladoras*.

Maquilapolis follows a narrative arc that builds to success for the women's campaign for environmental clean-up by major corporations and the remitting of severance pay for workers who were rendered unemployed when a factory closed—presumably to find a more profitable set of circumstances, partly through unpaid wages. The women's collective efforts to use mediamaking as a political tool reflects the ideals of the New Latin American Cinema movement of the 1960s—which included cross-border collaborations like *Raíces de sangre*—to use cinema to create social change. This movement coincides with the precepts of the Chicano and civil rights movements' emphasis on social justice and antiracism in the struggle for self-determination and equality. *Maquilapolis* fulfills these ideals for a new era in which economic instability leads to full blown crisis, the impact of which is more far ranging for the marginal and the poor on both sides of the border.

Women's Work

Regardless of the type of feminized labors, domestic or factory and sweatshop piecework, the gendering of labor is crucial to the development of immigration policy and to the production of the social mood about female migrants. A mostly female population is deemed a burden to the state for women's reproductive capacities and the associated costs of family and child care, education, and other public benefits and services. Thus policies and public attitudes shift attention from the labor performed by migrant women to their perceived economic burden as mothers. It is against this mood that Araceli, the protagonist of *Barbarian Nurseries*, as a domestic worker does not express affinity for children nor a desire to have her own or replicate the domestic scenario she services. Nonetheless, women are deemed burdens to the state, and their labors are further marginalized and unsecure.

Made in L.A. documents the plight of a number of women who work as seamstresses in sweatshops under inhumane and illegal conditions. They are paid less than minimum wage and are not paid overtime. And their bosses demand that they work ever faster and longer without breaks. These conditions recall that of the women doing similar work along the border in *Raíces de sangre*. What is immediately different about these two examples is partly genre-based—one is a fictional film and *Made in L.A.* is a documentary. But they share similar reality effects. There is a greater sense of time compression in more recent productions that take place during the intensification of globalization after NAFTA and in the lead up to and during the Great Recession. The women in *Made in L.A.* and *Maquilapolis* have less time to explore ways they might question their conditions. Their shift work often runs consecutively and overnight. In *Made in L.A.,* the workers are bleary eyed and fatigued but find time to meet at the *Centro de Trabajadores de Costura*. And the latter is run by Spanish-speaking Asian American activists, who remind us that Asians form part of the legacy of the trade and still constitute a fraction of workers—though the future of the trade is found in undocumented workers who face ever more precarious conditions and dehumanizing treatment.

Made in L.A. is about a group of women, workers and organizers, sometimes one and the same, that fight for fair wages and working conditions for seamstresses in sweatshops in L.A. The story centers around the "Forever 21" campaign that brought the owner of the company into negotiations with its underpaid and exploited workforce. This is not a story of immediate results or simple outcomes but one that took more than 36 months to accomplish—unlike, for example, the "Bread and Roses" campaign in the film of the same name that ended quickly and spectacularly, partly as a way of conveying all of the various steps and stages of such a campaign for audiences who may not otherwise consider activism as a viable option. *Made in L.A.* has a similar effect: it is ultimately successful, thus eliciting hope, while it also shows the struggle and minor setbacks along the way. And the story reflects the conditions for workers in crisis capitalism, that is, when conditions become ever more precarious and owners of companies ever more difficult to confront.

Undocumented migrants from Central America and Mexico replace sweatshop workers of a previous generation that came most often from East Asia. The Asian American organizers of the seamstresses, Joann Lo and Kimi Lee, cite this history as one that informs and inspires their own activist work. And in keeping with this shift in population, everyone associated with the *Centro de Trabajadores de Costura* speaks fluent Spanish. These women, and the women who assume leadership roles in the organization, exemplify what Gramsci calls "conscious leadership." They are as invested in the struggle for worker rights as they are in the cultivation of leaders within worker ranks who might replace or consolidate their leadership. Lo and Lee represent a form of cross-racial coalition against worker competition based on race. That is, those in the racial middle, Asian and Latino immigrants, have often been pit against each other in the labor market, though these groups also suffer equally from marginalization as racialized outsiders deemed foreign and unassimilable. Lo explains that her parents are immigrants who faced difficult conditions; her mother did not speak English, so she sees a "connection to the workers." Asian Americans are part of the garment worker labor history and certainly part of the labor activist present. This is in contradistinction to the example mentioned earlier from *Bread and Roses*, albeit Hollywood fare, in which the Anglo male organizer (Adrien Brody) is admonished by one of the workers he organizes, and with whom he becomes romantically involved, as having no true investment in their labor issues as a college-educated white man. Moreover, the collaboration of Asian and Latino workers reflects conditions of the labor market in major cities of the U.S. along with the geopolitics of companies from Asia that employ Latina and Latino workers—this is the case in both *Made in L.A.* and *Maquilapolis*.

Asians and Latinos constitute "disposable" and "deportable" subjects often deemed exterior to U.S. national identity and subject to expulsion. And immigration policy reflects this cultural attitude consistently from the Chinese Exclusion Act, the Gentleman's Agreement, to immigration quotas based on national origin. Nicholas de Genova notes the paradox of this condition of marginality for those in the "racial middle":

> To be Latino or Asian within the space of the U.S. nation-state or its imperial projects has, therefore, nearly always meant having one's specific national origins as well as cultural, religious, and linguistic particularities—in short, the convoluted amalgam of one's foreign or alien status—rendered virtually indistinguishable from a conclusively racial condition of non-whiteness. The additive elaboration of racial categories derived from terms that refer to, or may be associated with, supranational global regions—*Asian, Latino*—abides by the same

fundamental logic that racialized people in terms of their presumed affiliation with foreign *places*.[11]

Thus, like Latinos, Asians and Asian Americans alike are often seen as immigrants and deemed foreign. This sense of foreignness and marginality links the Asian American organizers with the Latina/o workers and activists.

The title of the documentary indicates both its local production and tacitly global distribution. "Made in L.A." suggests that something was fabricated or construed locally but might be consumed globally or further afield. And it points to how this conflict is formulated and meaningful in global cities of the U.S., cities that are local instances of global capitalism. The struggle between Central American and Mexican workers and the Korean owners of "Forever 21" could be dismissed as one limited to and relevant only to immigrants and foreigners. Yet it involves a known and widely consumed brand and store and impacts a much wider range of publics. Lee explains that the company does 95% of its production in Los Angeles, which makes it a key example in the struggle for labor rights in the city. The company is a fulcrum of local sweatshop practices, and a ruling against it would impact the larger urban community of workers and set standards that might be applied more globally. The campaign against the company targets everyone, small and large, in the chain of production and distribution and is itself a key example of activist strategy. In a telling scene, the organization pickets outside of a Forever 21 store in Los Angeles, drawing a large crowd of curious onlookers along with the workers and managers of the store. The shopkeepers stand on the sidelines and film the workers. An older white man sidles up to one of the Forever 21 shopkeepers with a camera and suggests that "instead of taking pictures" he tell the company that the workers have legitimate claims. The shop keep argues that they are targeting the wrong people, and his interlocutor contests that retailers "sidestep their responsibility" in a chain of deferrals and dismissals.

The documentary makes the story both part of the enduring local politics of sweatshops and part of a global movement, while it also is a sign of the diversity, power and number of Asian and Latino workers in the U.S. In the end, Lupita, one of the most vocal of the worker-activists, becomes an organizer at an international level. The story becomes her story; she is literally "made" or transformed in L.A. and sent all over the world to represent her fellow workers. The lawsuit against Forever 21 challenged the legality of the systemic use of sweatshop labor. And though it was initially dismissed, the appeal, after many months, was successful and would force the company to defend itself in court. The latter decides instead to enter into settlement negotiations. Part of the agreement includes that the company would ensure that its clothing would be made under lawful conditions, setting a precedent and standard for sweatshop practices.

The story does not lend itself to a simple coalition or conflict between Asians and Latinos for the complexity of each racialized and migrant group politics within the U.S. polity and economy. The business owners represent the mobility of capital and the deracination of money and consumer goods. The Korean owner of the company, Do Wang Chang, lives "like a king," according to his workers, in a Beverly Hills neighborhood secured and patrolled by police to protect the homeowners. The workers take their protest all the way up the chain to Chang's home and are casually questioned by police for their permits. The idea that Chang lives like a king foregrounds his sovereignty and the sovereignty of capital that moves freely and under the protection of the state. In contrast, the workers, as labor, are not free; their movement is limited and permanently visible, subject to surveillance.

Hollywood film and television culture glosses these contradictions and reconfigures them as productive of desire and fantasy. In "Devious Maids," the worker-boss dynamic is either eroticized and the origin of romance or a coalition of sisterly intimacy. And the world of the boss represents a world of consumer desires and social aspirations. In the activist-oriented documentaries, the boss-employee relationships are sites of negotiation, deep inequities, and signs of the social abyss between the global North and the migrant South. Coalitions, in the latter, are political formations in the service of freeing the worker from the confinement of their bodies and consciousness. The associations of workers are a step towards forms of agency and self-possession. The dehumanization these women face along with the atomization and alienation of the domestic space of work cannot be remedied with a fair wage or good working conditions. Financial or other forms of compensation do not neutralize the depredations of capitalism. Regardless of pay, caring for the family of an employer means alienation from one's own families, extended and immediate. While a powerful cross-border and cross-racial social movement for domestic worker rights has gained ground, the actual conditions of these kinds of labor, of feminized and female-targeted employment, reproduce racial and gender forms of capitalism. These texts point to the possibility of enduring coalitions between immigrant groups and across racialized populations. The connection between Asians and Latinos is part of the history of political organizing, and in the next chapter, it is deemed a future, in *Lunar Braceros*, of inevitable racial intimacies that reflects geopolitical affiliations across the global South.

Notes

1. Though men and non-gender conforming peoples also migrate for domestic work, they are often sidelined in studies that focus on cis-gender women performing feminine or feminized labors. See Martin Manalansan, "Queer

Intersections: Sexuality and Gender in Migration Studies." *IMR* 40:1 (2006) 224–249.
2. Mary Romero, Valerie Preston, and Wenona Giles. "Care Work in a Globalizing World." *When Care Work Goes Global: Locating the Social Relations of Domestic Work.* Eds. Mary Romero, Valerie Preston, and Wenona Giles (Surrey: Ashgate, 2014), 1.
3. Alicia Garza, "Afterword to the 2016 Edition." *Disposable Domestics: Immigrant Women Workers in the Global Economy.* Ed. Grace Chang (Chicago: Haymarket Books, 2016), 210–211.
4. Hector Tobar, *The Barbarian Nurseries* (New York: Farrar, Strauss and Giroux, 2011), 183.
5. Isabel Molina Guzmán, *Dangerous Curves: Latina Bodies in the Media* (New York: New York University Press, 2010).
6. Irene Mata, *Domestic Disturbances: Reimagining Narratives of Gender, Labor, and Immigration* (Austin: University of Texas Press, 2014), 23.
7. Tobar, 43.
8. Mary Romero, *Maid in the U.S.A.* (New York: Routledge, 1992), 15.
9. Melissa W. Wright, "Public Women, Profit, and Femicide in Northern Mexico." *South Atlantic Quarterly* 105:4 (2006) 688 [681–698].
10. www.maquilapolis.com/project_eng.htm
11. Nicholas de Genova, *Racial Transformations: Latinos and Asians Remaking the United States.* Ed. Nicholas de Genova (Durham: Duke University Press, 2006), 12.

3   Border Futures

Maquilapolis ends just after the 2001 economic crisis that followed the attack on the World Trade Center. While the workers wage a successfully binational campaign to obligate a factory to clean up its toxic waste dump along the border and fight to receive their due severance from Sanyo, they nonetheless face an uncertain future. Their precariousness is a consequence of larger cycles of economic crisis. Companies seeking to pay lower wages move their factories to Southeast Asia. And these women, once "surplus labor," are now simply a "surplus population" straining the infrastructure of a city that did not develop to accommodate the workers it demanded.[1] The 2009 speculative novel by Rosaura Sánchez and Beatrice Pita *Lunar Braceros 2125–2148* imagines a different future for the displaced and disposable borderlands workers. They are sent to a new frontier zone of all that is considered extraneous and unincorporable: the moon. And space, as we know from popular "Star Trek" and *Star Wars* storylines, is the final frontier for human life and labor.

After the crises of the present, the future is the border. At least that is the case in *Sleep Dealer* (2008), *Lunar Braceros 2125–2148*, and the future border city, Santa Teresa, designed by architect Fernando Romero. Taken together, these texts present a future of integrated networks in which the border is not just actual but temporal, separating the present time of crisis and migrant phobia and a future of networked mobility and new forms of human interaction and settlement. The border is paradoxically the site of the past of U.S. manufacturing and the future of neoliberal capitalism. And the outcomes of capitalism for the marginalized and migrant communities are catastrophes of various kinds, ones that persist without remedy in the present and for which these texts imagine a different possible future.

Sleep Dealer (2008) enacts the dystopic science fiction world of a film like *Day Without a Mexican* (2004) in which the global North never lacks for the labor that sustains it nor do they have to contend with the physical and political presence of the migrant worker. As a genre, science fiction literalizes the symbologies of fiction, in this case literalizing the fantasies of Anglo-Americans who want all the work without the workers. This is also the new condition of capitalism in which temporary labor is also the unseen labor of workers who might literally work from home in their home countries—much like call center workers who support and care for the technologically distressed in the global North from Manila, Delhi, or Mexico City.

In *Sleep Dealer*, the workers toil in their sleep. Their unconscious minds are activated by machines and connected to a global circuit through which they labor remotely. The digital world is somatized and integrated into bodily experiences; it takes over consciousness, rendering its subjects unconscious and putting them in a sleep-like state. It is risky and precarious work. The workers become more and more denatured and closer to the eternal sleep of death, even risking death if their minds are over-leveraged or mined beyond their capacity.

The storyline follows a group of interconnected characters drawn together in some cases by their virtual linkages. The main character, Memo, lives in a remote village in Mexico where he hacks into a secure network to spy on government military operations in the U.S. In a story inflected with the history of *campesino* struggles in the Americas, Memo's family's land and its natural resource, water, has been ceded and privatized by corporate powers who sell back the water to the family at astronomical rates. Memo hacks into the government site that puts water activists like his father under surveillance and keeps track of their water holdings in government protected sites, revealing a clear corporate-military alliance. Memo is targeted as a security risk and subject to a drone strike that incinerates his father, initiating his forced migration north to Tijuana to seek work to support his family. Ironically, this and other drone attacks are part of a reality TV show upon which Memo's brother is fixated. This scenario recalls events in Central America in the 1980s when paramilitary attacks protecting landholder interests forced entire populations from their native lands to the north in Mexico and the United States—reflected in the film *El Norte* (1983). And it echoes similar stories of economic exile from debt-addled Mexico during the same era, phobically depicted in Hollywood fare like *The Border* (1982) or *Borderline* (1980).

The condition of migration is highly mediated and creates a number of ancillary products and commodities. For example, on the bus North, Memo meets Luz, a writer who traffics in stories about the marginalized population in the border zone of Tijuana. He recounts his tragic story, which she promptly turns into a downloadable commodity. The story links Memo to the drone pilot who killed Memo's father. The pilot is Luz's first consumer of the Memo line of non-fiction. He buys into her site to assuage his guilt and find a way to make amends. Meanwhile Luz deepens her intimacy with

Memo to mine his memory for more marketable stories. Memo's work occurs on the same register for each of his two "bosses," in both cases his unconscious is an exploitable resource as a store of both memory and of mental labors.

Todo el Trabajo sin los Trabajadores

Lysa Rivera situates *Sleep Dealer* as part of borderland science fiction after NAFTA, after what Guillermo Gómez Peña designates as the "new world border" or the "fourth world of utopian borderlessness."[2] She finds that cultural producers use science fiction to "articulate experiences not only of alienation, displacement, and marginalization but also those of survival, resistance, and resilience."[3] Science fiction as Chicano futurism takes the current conditions of migrant labor to their logical end and exposes the subsequent contradictions therein, forcing the reader or audience to confront the unhappy conditions in the future created by the present social order. Curtis Marez analyzes the film in terms of the futurism of the agribusiness development model based on mechanization as one model that demands work without workers. Agribusiness futurism disseminated surveillance technologies and visual media to manage and control workers. Marez argues that, ultimately, farm workers would commandeer media and visual culture to resist the forces of dehumanization and change "*what* audiences saw" and "alter *how* they saw agribusiness." They would generate a different ethic and aesthetic that he describes as "farm worker futurism."[4] Like Romero with his future border city, farm worker futurism imagines and projects an alternate and more equitable future.

In addition to being post-NAFTA, *Sleep Dealer* explores the conjunction of science fiction and the borderlands imaginary in the time of deepening crisis just before the economic freefall of 2008. And the book's release during the year of the crash makes this text ever more significant as a reflection on the dehumanizing effects of capitalism. The Great Recession completely disoriented the middle and lower middle classes in the U.S. who lost their homes and jobs and had to seek new ways of supporting themselves. The crisis impacted migrant communities differently; it did not reshape the world but intensified conditions for migrant labor and made these conditions intractable and relentless, without recourse or alternate means of survival. And activism against neoliberalism is deemed tantamount to terrorism—as in the case of Memo's father whose protests against the ceding of water-rich land was construed as "aqua-terrorism."

Sleep Dealer suggests that the condition along the border represents the combined past of U.S. labor in general and manufacturing in particular and the future of the social order of neoliberalism. The economic crisis of

2008 was preceded by a downturn in manufacturing; the latter was replaced by services, including those related to finance, insurance, and real estate (FIRE). This initiated the rise of finance or the financialization of the economy, the restructuring of economic dynamics through the deregulation of markets or through neoliberalism. Geoff Mann provides a succinct history of this shift, noting the "birthday" of neoliberalism in the 1979 Volcker interest rate hike that made investment in plants and brick and mortar businesses too costly and encouraged businesses to get creative about profit seeking. Businesses seeking reduction in overhead costs turned to financialized products to increase revenues. Financial securities spread investment risk over several kinds of products and across different regions, sectors, and temporalities.[5] For example, futures trading, betting on the future price of a commodity or currency, meant that the future might not be predictable, but it could certainly be bet against to present the illusion of certainty in the face of the unknown.

Border science fiction narratives mark the importance of the "birthday" of neoliberalism when the actual work of U.S. industry, manufacturing, slips below the border to be replaced by the speculative fictions of finance. But manufacturing remains a vital part of the U.S. imagination, particularly around public debates about trade and migrant labor. Manufacturing is a source of ambivalence; it is both the irksome wage labor of the past and a nostalgic signifier of stable work within a growing economy. The border crosser as worker is the sign of this contradiction as a figure that helps expand the economy and an intrusive sign of a racialized future, that is, a sign of the decline of white supremacy. The Mexican labor force in the U.S. is shaped by the history of the *bracero* as a male worker, a consequence of popular culture and policy, who is used to meet labor deficits then, when no longer needed, expelled at state will. On the other side of this labor dynamic is the *maquiladora* worker, imagined as a female, and the feminized labor market. She haunts the U.S. from below the border as part of an unseen workforce who manufacture the commodities and technologies of everyday U.S. life. The *maquila* workers remain south of the border while their migrant counterparts move north as a mobile and, within the history of labor activism, mobilizing force. *Sleep Dealer* shifts this dynamic by immobilizing all Mexican workers and stemming the flow of migration of men and women in border towns. Mexican workers can participate in the work of building the U.S.—Memo takes a job in construction—but they will not have access to the vital political spaces of organizing for fair wages and working conditions. They risk losing their jobs and income with so many workers eager to replace those who protest too much.

Sleep Dealer conveys the future of speculative capitalism by flattening the metaphors associated with it. The idea of working at a distance or working virtually, online or even through robots and other mediations, is a present reality rather than the imaginings of a speculative future. Yet science fiction literalizes the metaphors of virtuality. The human body is the virtual world; it is enmeshed in the digital networks rather than outside of it as an agent operating it. And labor, like capital, is capable of being overleveraged. This is a different kind of dystopia than that imagined in Post-Fordism. In the latter, humans are replaced by machines. During the intensification of globalization in the 1980s, the border was a locus of the various outcomes and consequences of this process. The rapid industrialization of border cities in Mexico resulted in human rights crises and ecological disasters that only worsened with the passing of the North American Free Trade Agreement (NAFTA). The concern with immigration as a "flood" or "tidal wave" and other metaphors of natural disaster symbolically off-loaded the various disasters that the global North enacted upon the borderlands onto the body of the migrant. And it alluded to the idea that disaster, incarnate, might be mobile or mobilizable. Likewise, the idea that labor would be downsized and replaced by machines is associated with the diminished and downgraded work of policing and security rather than the more ubiquitous worker oppression in border *maquiladoras.*

The character and quality of labor in the 1980s signified very differ-ently across each side of the dividing line. For example, in Hollywood films like those mentioned earlier—*Borderline, The Border*, and *Flash-point* (1984)—Anglo border patrolmen are underpaid and overextended workers subject to various kinds of strain and fatigue. Their safety and livelihood are threatened by the lack of human resources and respect for their labor. And in some storylines, like *Flashpoint*, they are replaced by the return of surveillance technologies from the Vietnam War which will render them obsolete and out of work or physically inert managers of machines.[6] Machines replace Anglo workers, who become unemployed much like their counterparts and kin in Great Recession popular culture. They are put out of work, rendered useless by austerity policies and ideas about worker and workplace efficiency. This occasions, in contemporary narratives, a redoubling of efforts to regain economic solvency and a turn to creative enterprise to do so. In 1980s border films, Anglo border cops resist their own downsizing and work within a system that constrains the execution of their responsibilities. They prove their mettle by humane interpretations of their duties and go against the law to better shape it to their liberal purposes. They prove their worth as sympathetic characters who return babies to migrant mothers, allow undocumented workers to continue working, and help the helpless. Hollywood border films instill in the audience the idea that these Anglo heroes are humans that should not be replaced by machines.

At the same time, in the 1980s, on the other side of the border, labor is mechanized and workers are reduced to functional machines who must be more efficient; they must manufacture more in less time and for less remuneration in a steady erosion of wages and benefits. Workers, particularly women, are subject to endless cycles of turnover and disposability. Speculative fictions explore not the potential of technological progress but how this "progress" ensures the foreclosure of a future for migrant workers as fully human subjects and agents. *Sleep Dealer* literalizes Anglo and mainstream U.S. desire to have the benefits of labor without the irksome presence of the worker or the possibility that the migrant might become an immigrant or that the guest worker might become a permanent resident and move towards gaining the entitlements and responsibilities of citizenship. The film exposes the imperial desire to expand production and development of the global North while maintaining a system of racial capitalism based in imperialism and white supremacy. The expansion of an internal labor market comprised of racialized outsiders poses threats to white mastery. The novel *Lunar Braceros* shows how the unchecked expansion of neoliberal capitalism challenges the symbolic boundary between the global North and the global South. Instead, the novel redraws the lines between nations and generates a different political order, one that is ruled by corporate interests across racial and ethnic lines.

Lunar Braceros moves the story of borderland migrant workers into the not-so-distant future of 2125 when *braceros* are required for lunar transport of toxic and other forms of waste from the earth. The *braceros* are also technologically proficient "hands-on workers who [can] adapt to changing lunar situations" and are "capable of solving unforeseen problems."[7] The novel, narrated by Lydia, recounts the past of a world that takes place in the future within "The Great Political Restructuring" that created the new nation-state of Cali-Texas which, like Romero's future geopolitical borderland city, is comprised of an integration of former Northern Mexican states (Tamaulipas, Coahuila, Chihuahua, Nuevo Leon, Sonora, and Baja California), former U.S. southwestern states (Texas, Colorado, New Mexico, Arizona, Utah, California, and Nevada), and former U.S. states in the Pacific Rim (Oregon, Washington, Alaska, and Hawai'i). And in a prescient critique of trade agreements like the defunct TransPacific Partnership that would have consolidated U.S. economic hegemony, this new alliance emerges from "transnational agri-business corporations and the four big bio-techs, companies that controlled anything and everything that had to do with technology transfer, informatics and any kind of power generation, bio-fuel, nuclear or otherwise."[8] Also the historical references suggest a circularity of history and inevitable return of issues besetting marginalized labor, including the persistence and expansion of colonialism, precarity, and the co-opting of political coalitions by corporate capitalism. Rivera argues that the novel is an example of post-NAFTA border science fiction in its preoccupations with labor, global capitalism, exploitation and resistance within colonial border histories. The novel is also about the ratcheting up and proliferation of forms of violence as and through racial capitalism, particularly a form that collapses histories and regions to increase the influence of capitalism and its information technologies. And the nation-state is, as mentioned earlier, a geopolitical instantiation of empire. As activists seek ways to link across regions and racialized groups, the state as empire forges similar coalitions and, in this possible world, nearly forecloses interventions into or transformations of the imperial order.

Lydia tells of a disposable population left behind by this political reordering. They are all manner of people of color and the economically dispossessed who are shuttled onto reservations. The "reservation" no longer designates the particular experience of Native Americans but anyone who is marginal and expendable.

THE RESERVATIONS WERE AND ARE A TYPE OF POPULA-
TION CONTROL CAMP MECHANISM. THEY WERE STARTED
TO KEEP THE HOMELESS AND THE UNEMPLOYED OFF THE
STREETS AND OFF WELFARE. IN THE RESERVATION WE
WERE REQUIRED TO WORK AT ASSIGNED TASKS; SOME
HAD JOBS IN NUCLEAR WEAPON INDUSTRIES, CHEMICAL
LABS, AND MORE ROUTINE INDUSTRIES. THE SKILL-LESS
WERE MADE TO MAINTAIN THE STREETS. UNEMPLOYED
TEACHERS WERE REQUIRED TO TEACH IN THE RESERVA-
TION SCHOOLS. UNEMPLOYED NURSES AND DOCTORS
WERE REQUIRED TO WORK IN THE RESERVATION CLINICS.
THE RESERVATIONS WERE REALLY A TYPE OF PRISON, SUR-
ROUNDED BY A RAZOR WIRE FENCE THAT COULD EASILY
BE CUT OR EVEN JUMPED. BUT RARELY DOES ANYONE TRY.
WE KNEW AS KIDS THAT BEYOND A CLEARING THERE WERE
PATROLS AND THAT IF YOU WERE CAUGHT TRYING TO RUN
AWAY YOU COULD BE KILLED ON THE SPOT.[9]

Just as surveillance shapes the entire social order marking no distinction between the reservation and its exterior, so does the status of expendability or disposability shape those in the margins, people of color and the economically distressed. The only escape from these proto-prisons is to volunteer to work as a cyber-*bracero* on the moon, yet they discover that workers are eliminated so that the corporations do not have to bear the cost of their transport back to earth. The narrator and her colleagues on the moon plan an insurrection to halt this barbaric practice.

The sections of the novel that appear in all capital letters are notes in direct address from the narrator to her son and give clear explanations of the conditions in the New Imperial Order. The typesetting of these sections adds a sense of urgency and expediency to their meaning. It intensifies the sense of fear and suffering of the imagined speaker while, at each appearance, it marks the transformation of her political orientation towards a liberatory future. The last of Lydia's entries ends with a shift from the personal register to a political exhortation:

> THIS IS NOT MERELY A PERSONAL THING, NOT AN INDIVIDUAL BATTLE, ALTHOUGH I HAVE MUCH TO RESENT. IT WILL BE A COLLECTIVE STRUGGLE, A CLASS STRUGGLE. WHAT PACOMIO TRIED TO DO OH SO MANY CENTURIES AGO, THE INDIANS IN CHINGANAZA HAVE ACHIEVED AND NOW WE TOO MUST ATTAIN THIS FREEDOM FROM EXPLOITATION ON THE RESERVATIONS IN CALI-TEXAS. CHINGANAZA WILL SERVE AS INSPIRATION FOR FUTURE CHANGES IN CALI-TEXAS. OUR STRUGGLE WILL BE THE BEGINNING OF A DIFFERENT WORLD.[10]

This final entry links the struggles and worker crises diachronically to expose the cycle and ongoing struggle against oppression, one that persists into the future and one in which the future, though ever more oppressive, nonetheless contains the possibility for successful resistance and social transformation. This struggle, Lydia suggests earlier, must originate and take place at a local level and expand centrifugally. She documents her political efforts to organize and create a global movement through digital networks, yet one that deteriorates into inert scholarly discourse:

> Those of us on the Left that survived the Cali-Texas purges . . . began again to organize, this time more solidly in terms of a global movement that synchronized local cells though alternative internet systems that piggybacked clandestinely on the worldwide communication grid. In this way we were able to reach even the farthest village in Africa and Asia. I got involved with a small group at the university, but as time went on I found the group to be more academic and theoretical than involved in praxis.[11]

This leads her to local protests on a smaller scale that are so effective that she is detained and sentenced to prison for her political resistance, for which she is deemed, like Memo's father in *Sleep Dealer*, to be a "terrorist." When she is released, she is put into the proto-carceral holding pens of "reservations." Once she is shipped out as a lunar *bracero*, her activist work becomes interplanetary, and by writing her thoughts down for future generations, emblematized by the son to whom it is addressed, it becomes future directed and transhistorical.

Border as Future

These futuristic stories reveal that with each turn on the capitalist cycle, with each crisis and resolution, social inequity only deepens. The border is a powerful model of global capitalism. The social order is re-imagined through the border economies. We witness the *bracero*-ification of all workers—in *Sleep Dealer* these workers are still of Mexican origin, whereas *Lunar Braceros* imagines this condition of unsecured laboring for all marginalized groups. This follows the mood and cycle of crisis and complacency. The border economies represent the permanent condition of crisis of economic circumstances that steadily decline and worsen and in which the ultimate outcome is genocide. The lunar company assigns less value to the laboring bodies than the products of their labor. These bodies are disposed of to avoid incurring the cost of their return transport to earth. The border economy is evident in the extraction of resources, human and mineral, and it signals the end of the capitalist line and its ultimate future. This resounds with the idea of space as the "final frontier," as the limit and end of capitalist expansion. The moon is the place of last resort after the expansion of U.S. boundaries into the Pacific—exemplified in the inclusion of Hawai'i into the major imperial state of Cali-Texas and in the ideological frame of trade agreements like CAFTA-DR or the defunct TransPacific Partnership—in the coalition of powerful states.

The question that these texts pose is multiplex. They imagine a future of more, not less, imperial prowess from the global North. They make the future of capitalism the future of the border. And they pose questions about political organization, particularly in *Lunar Braceros*, from the vantage point of a future beyond the civil rights movements of the 1960s and 1970s. That is, they question whether the future yields political progress or better and more effective remedies for social ills. The various anti-racist movements like *el movimiento* were co-opted by the state, particularly in educational institutions, and turned into "multiculturalism" as a sign of the United States' exemplarity and exceptionalism through liberal democracy. Direct action, protests, and sit-ins, for example, gave way to curricular reform and rhetoric about political and cultural representation. One could imagine the multicultural state becoming Cali-Texas or some other coalition of marginalized groups that, as in the novel, perform the bidding of a mainstream political elite. Thus the future dystopic border that is a present condition for many in the region and for those living in the margins would become the state of things for the entire imperial nation. The economic crisis of 2008 that exposed the rapaciousness of capitalism generated activist movements against it that soon gave way to the idea that a renewed and revised form of capitalism, greenwashed and more humane, would provide solutions and remedies for the poor and the dispossessed.

Speculative fiction literally puts the future in the present. It imagines a future wildly out of joint with the present but shaped by its major coordinates. The main tropes of these border tales are neo-liberal labor dynamics, the crises inherent to and created by capitalism, and the role of the border and Mexico in the U.S. economy. The border, often deemed a place of separation, is presented as a site of integration, as the locus of global capitalism. Speculative fiction takes the capital formations at the border to their logical end, often by tracing the impact of this future upon the narrative world.

Much like speculative fictions, architect Fernando Romero rethinks the separation of national spaces at the border to imagine an integrated and "super-connected" walking city that spans both sides of the U.S.-Mexico border. Romero unveiled the plans for a speculative binational city called Santa Teresa at the 2016 London Design Biennale. The city is the conglomeration of three communities: Santa Teresa, New Mexico; San José and San Jerónimo, Chihuahua. In this complex multi-nodal plan, the border is the sign of the future. It is where political impasses and economic crises of the present might be remedied through creativity and integrative processes. This imagined city is the culmination of a border futures project outlined in a longer presentation of the history and future of the border in Romero's *Hyperborder*. The latter does what border scholars and border studies in general have done for years, which is to examine the U.S.-Mexico border as both extraordinary—as a site of surveillance, low-intensity war, and clashing cultures and economies—and as a case study and model for all borders. Romero examines the border as a model for the future and future space of global integration. *Hyperborder* refers to the various economic, political and cultural possibilities of borderland integration along with the historical conditions of interdependence already evident in sister cities along the border like San Diego and Tijuana or the two Laredos. For instance, the sister cities of Ciudad Juárez and El Paso, called the border's "metroplex," are key nodes in a system of interconnection and interdependence.[12] They are linked through a number of issues, from environmental concerns and shared resources to trade, tourism, circular migration, and other forms of communication.

In *Hyperborder*, Romero offers a background and overview of the history of Latinos in the U.S. and their continued influence and impact in what William V. Flores and Rita Benmayor call "cultural citizenship" or the marking of place and belonging through cultural means.[13] He notes what he calls "future scenarios" around several topics including security, economies, transportation, migration, education, and urbanization. In a sense, this work is a primer for a readership with little knowledge of Latinos in the U.S. or the history of the relationship of the United States and Mexico. Like *Lunar Braceros*, *Hyperborder* predicts a future that is the border. Romero's fully integrated transborder city, Santa Teresa, is the utopic version of Cali-Texas, environmentally sustainable and generative of equality through ease of access for all of its inhabitants. He cites architectural and design firm James Corner Field Operations' creative plan that proposes integrating the extant border security apparatus with a "continuous energy harnessing strip" to create a "renewable energy generator."[14] The transborder city might accommodate growth and reflect and project urban futures that build from extant infrastructure. Romero's plan for urban growth includes a process of integration:

As the border population is expected to double by the year 2020, addressing urbanization in the region will require sustainable growth. Installing sewage and water infrastructure between sister cities, attracting new talent to border communities, improving the use of public space and funds for a higher standard of living, and creating binational housing plans should be integral parts of the future urban development processes at the border.[15]

New forms of urbanization will be shaped by and anticipate binational migration. *Hyperborder* prophesies possible futures along the border pointing to outcomes that would logically follow from the current order of things and that tacitly suggest alternatives or remedies. These prophesies read like headlines: "Not American but Angeleno. Secession Movement Spreads Like Wildfire across the Globe's Major Cities." Global cities will be sovereign states. This headline prefaces a discussion of the need for cooperation to build binational infrastructure for water and sewage systems that would operate more efficiently and sustainably. Such would be the case for other forms of development that would reduce North-South imbalances and ameliorate conditions that give rise to undocumented migration. The call to denationalize border cities and officially recognize their biregional, binational, and biracial status would change the dynamic between the United States and Mexico and shift the xenophobic discourses emanating from the global North. He prophesies that undocumented immigration to the U.S. will decline by granting binational status to border cities.

As border cities such as El Paso-Cd. Juárez and San Diego-Tijuana are granted binational status, border crossings from one country to another will be expedited thanks to a joint police force and customs and immigration agency. Although residents of these cities will not be granted double citizenship, permits for anyone without a criminal record to work on either side of the border will be issued within the next six months. Workers who in the past might have wanted to enter the U.S. illegally are expected to settle in the Mexican areas of these cities and apply for binational work permits instead. Many workers may not even need to cross the border to seek employment, since the official recognition of the binational status of these border cities is expected to create at least ten thousand new jobs, mainly in the city services sector.[16]

This idea about binational integration is the basis of the speculative plan of Santa Teresa called "Border City," designed by Romero's team at his firm, FR-EE and pictured in Image 3.1.

The city is comprised of interlocking hexagrams with various nodes or hubs and intersecting diagonal lines of communication linking the exterior to the interior. FR-EE's website explains the proposed design:

> Border City presents a vision for a binational city on one of the world's most important borders, that of the United States and Mexico, whose

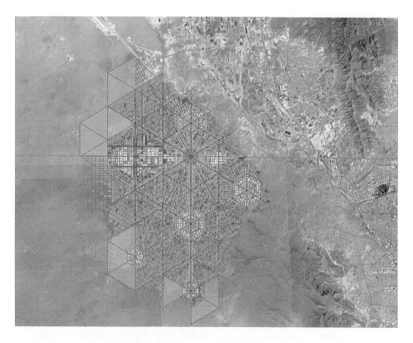

Image 3.1 FR-EE Plan for Transborder City Santa Teresa

boundary states are now home to over 100 million people. The concept is rooted in the long history of places where frontiers meet, cities where cultures clash and blend. This integrated master plan is conducive to both sides of the border, drawing upon industrial, employment and trade opportunities, while recognizing shortcomings in urban planning. Romero's urban prototype, with a hexagonal plan, might offer a new model for cities as populations grow, migration increases, and economies continue to globalise.[17]

It is not sufficient to rethink, repurpose, or redeem a space; it has to be completely reconfigured to reflect the non-hierarchical spatialization of binationalism. In U.S. mass and popular culture, the United States and Mexico are depicted as places of contrast in a manner that derives from colonial discourses. In Hollywood film and television culture, Mexico is continually represented as a nation beset by colonial decadence and racial degeneration. This is evident across the divided visual landscape of border films like *Touch of Evil* (1958), *The Border*, and *Traffic* (2000), in which the U.S. is developed and civilized while Mexico is backwards and unruly and associated with the past of the U.S. in its visual accordance with landscapes of the old West. A common visual trope that conveys the desirability of the U.S. in relation to Mexico is evident in the long line of stalled cars waiting, as if in a parking lot, for entry into the U.S. while a sparse number of cars and trucks cruise unobstructed southward. Romero redesigns these depictions, eliminates them, replacing an image of imbalance and inequality with one of integration. And this image of equity and collaboration might proliferate and expand to challenge the blockages and disruptions of barriers and fortified walls. The border is not a symbolic dividing line but a point of departure for post-national urban development. The line between nations becomes the focus and center of new cities. Santa Teresa is a model and master plan for other bordered cities and a new speculative landscape for a different border future—different, that is, from that of the science fiction stories. The future border has the potential to reshape hemispheric power dynamics and forestall the degradations of capitalism by building, as Romero proposes, integrated cities and bridges, not walls.

Notes

1. Alicia Schmidt-Camacho, "Ciudadana X: Gender Violence and the Denationalization of Women's Rights in Ciudad Juárez, Mexico." *The New Centennial Review* 5:1 (2005) 255–292.
2. Guillermo Gómez Peña, *The New World Border: Prophesies, Poems, & Loqueras for the End of the Century* (San Francisco: City Lights, 1996).
3. Lysa Rivera, "Future Histories and Cyborg Labor: Reading Borderlands Science Fiction after NAFTA." *Science Fiction Studies* 39:3 (2012) 415 [415–436].

4. Curtiz Marez, *Farm Worker Futurism: Speculative Technologies of Resistance* (Minneapolis: University of Minnesota Press, 2016), ix.
5. Geoff Mann, *Disassembly Required: A Field Guide to Actually Existing Capitalism* (Oakland: AK Press, 2013).
6. See Camilla Fojas, *Border Bandits: Hollywood on the Southern Frontier* (Austin: University of Texas Press, 2008).
7. Rosaura Sanchez and Beatrice Pita, *Lunar Braceros 2125–2149* (National City, Califas: Calaca Press, 2009), 6.
8. *Lunar Braceros*, 6–7.
9. Ibid, 13–14.
10. Ibid, 118.
11. Ibid, 34.
12. Fernando Romero, *Hyperborder: The Contemporary U.S.-Mexico Border and its Future* (New York: Princeton Architectural Press, 2007), 95.
13. William V. Flores and Rita Benmayor, *Latino Cultural Citizenship: Claiming Identity, Space, and Rights* (Boston: Beacon, 1997).
14. Ibid, 228–29.
15. Romero, 270.
16. Ibid, 280.
17. FR-EE.org.

Epilogue
Beyond Security

The border is the future. The inequity between border cities on each side of the international line is a consequence of distinct forms and representations of capitalism: one depicted as unhindered by regulation and the other as the consequence of a "law and order" regime based on the regulation of bodies and goods. These conditions represent the dark future of capital, particularly leading up to and just following the economic crisis of 2008 when social and economic disparities deepened. The Great Recession is not directly indexed in many of the post-crisis borderland narratives but is evoked in representations of the state of permanent crisis and emergency at the border. For geographer Reese Jones this mood is a consequence of the War on Terror as a conflict that creates and defines the "enemy other" as a dangerous threat and as "an evil that has no place in the modern world."[1] As a result, the state is defensive, violent, and exclusionary. The borderlands are at the edge of state authority where the nation must delimit its boundaries and make its sovereignty legible. State sovereignty is literally written on and in the wall.

Along the border, the machinery and institutions of capitalism expand under the alibi of security. Security is capitalized as a profitable outcome of crisis. Thus, there are two border economies. North of the border, in the United States, is a complex integrated security apparatus that links several local and national agencies to generate the multi-nodal corporate and government alliance of the security industrial complex. This regime is one that is poised to provide remedies for economic crises, creating massive human resource demands, and continually expanding to create capacity to process undocumented migrants and stem the flow of contraband goods.

The future border model of transborder integration promises economic expansion, but it is not as profitable as the current U.S. system of security capitalism. Todd Miller describes this as Border Patrol Capitalism and explores how the border security industry expanded exponentially as the frontline of the war on drugs after the signing of the North American Free

50   *Epilogue*

Trade Agreement (NAFTA). The border is the site of a sophisticated integration of surveillance technologies from watch towers, helicopters, night vision scopes, radar, drones and a number of other technologies under development by a conglomerate of border security companies clustered in the University of Arizona Science and Technology Park or Tech Park. The U.S.-Mexico border is a security laboratory for the rest of the world that represents billions of dollars in corporate investment and government contracts. Bruce Wright, the associate vice president of Tech Park describes the promise of the border security industry:

> There is a worldwide market for border technology. I mean there's the border between Ukraine and Russia, between Poland and Russia, between the Palestinians and the Israelis . . . all around the world, there are border issues.[2]

Border security policy and analysis focuses on the U.S.-Mexico border for the assumed fixity of the "natural" geographical delimitation of the Rio Grande/Rio Bravo. And border walls calcify symbolic boundaries to make them appear natural and immovable. In their analysis of border wall construction, David Carter and Paul Poast note that of the 62 border walls erected since 1800, a large number, 28, were built after 2000. They argue that "aggressive state strategy to manage border instability is on the rise."[3] A wall seems to address military and security demands, yet Carter and Poast argue that, on the contrary, it signals a demand for economic security. Walls symbolize the protection of national labor markets. And walls are merely the iconography of a "strong state" since borders are not static places on the ground. Saskia Sassen describes the current condition of borders as mobile and disaggregate, as proliferating and deracinated from geopolitical terrain.[4] The border is not just the natural barrier of the Rio Grande or a place upon which a wall or fence might be erected, but a diffuse space that appears everywhere that travel happens, in airports, roads, in the air and on the sea.

The border wall is the prevailing rhetorical device in discussions about restricting migrant labor. Sandro Mezzadra and Brett Neilson argue that the focus on walls as the paradigmatic symbol designates borders as sites of exclusion and expulsion. They explore the border as a mode of thinking and analysis or "border as method" to open up new ways of exploring dynamics of power and capital: "shedding light on the intermingling of sovereignty and governability and on the logistical operations underlying global circuits of accumulation."[5] Capitalism in crisis is nowhere more apparent than along the border and is best elucidated in relation to borders and migration, particularly in relation to the value and objectification of labor. Migration and mobility transform the meaning of labor and demand a rethinking of the relationship of citizen-worker to the state to imagine "new forms of political subjectivity."[6]

The U.S.-Mexico border contains all of the paradoxes and contradictions of capitalism in crisis. It is an actual geopolitical limit and it is the anxious sign of limitlessness. It is the line separating the North from its capitalist unconscious, its chaotic extremes and contradictions, subject to heavy policing and control. From its earliest depictions, the borderlands have been a space of disquiet and unrest that cannot be easily remedied. It conveys a reality of capitalism as generative of crisis, violence, and disorder. For Žižek violence is the result of the smooth operation of capitalism, not, as it has been characterized, as the result of cycles of instability.[7] Cedric Robinson describes this more accurately as racial capitalism or how capitalism originates in racial subjugation through slavery, imperialism, colonialism, and genocide.[8] The ongoing crisis and violence of racial capitalism is part of the social and cultural dynamics of border economies. Alicia Schmidt Camacho argues that this violence is inherent to the governing of the borderlands space, in the state and its policing forces.[9] Border economies hold tight to capitalist modes of production; they undergo crises but persist because border security is big business.

The border security apparatus dovetails with the carceral complex that includes hundreds of detention centers, many privately run, making big business of arresting, detaining, incarcerating, and deporting undocumented migrants.[10] Miller characterizes the system concisely as one energized by imagined fears; "The border security market is in an 'unprecedented boom period,' to use the words of one recent forecast, and the more danger, real or perceived, the better business has become."[11] The industry is fueled by the production of migrants as the objects of fear. It creates security in the form of assurances of border protection and jobs in the border patrol industrial complex. In fact, Customs and Border Protection, under the Department of Homeland Security, is the largest federal law enforcement agency, employing thousands under its auspices. Dismantling this vast capitalist structure and integrated network seems difficult if not impossible. Such is the bold plan of Romero's transborder city of Santa Teresa.

The utopic city plan by FR-EE of Santa Teresa would diminish security concerns at the border and decriminalize migrancy through the integration of transborder commercial, industrial, and consumer economies. This plan would dismantle border security capitalism by abolishing its prime commodities: security and disposable migrants—that is, notwithstanding James Corner Field Operations' proposal to integrate the extant border security apparatus with a "continuous energy harnessing strip." While Santa Teresa is a possible future, a viable plan, and a gesture to equity between Mexico and the United States, it is not welcome, nor readily considered in Washington.

The reason is simple, it is not a design that would support and enhance the hegemonic position of the colossus of the North. This plan is impossible under U.S. leadership that privileges the security industrial complex over diplomacy and social transformation. This future is stalled but perhaps it is not foreclosed. Romero's plan requires imagining the borderlands as common ground of the United States and Mexico, rather than opposing regimes. It would enable and legitimize migrant mobility within the transborder space of both nations. The space is designed to maximize access and mobility and the migrant is a defining member of this space. Romero imagines the border as a space of creativity not security, one capable of redefining governmentality in neoliberal capitalism.

The border is a point of departure for rethinking boundaries and barriers. Victor Konrad and John Everitt explore the literal fluidity of U.S. borders in the maritime boundary zones "where waters connect more than they divide."[12] They take as points of departure the 2011 security policy realignment between former U.S. President Obama and former Canadian Prime Minister Harper. They mobilize the metaphor of the fluid border as a perimeter to move beyond the literalness and linearity of borders to a notion of the borderlands as places of connection and interdependence. The maritime perimeter is a useful model for understanding borders as not just fluid but diffuse and capacious. This place of exchange and interaction highlights the cooperation between nations. The U.S.-Mexico border as the template and model of border studies is the place through which borders might be best resignified. It is the ultimate workshop for exploring the various practices of the security state and it is a stage for rethinking those same practices.

The border maintains a flexible theoretical economy even as the economic principles applied to it by Washington are intractable and calcified. In their seminal work on borderlands, Pekka Hämäläinen and Samuel Truett maintain a sense of the open possibility at the horizon of nations;

> If frontiers were the places where we once told our master American narratives, then borderlands are the places where those narratives come unraveled. They are ambiguous and often-unstable realms where boundaries are also crossroads, peripheries are also central places, homelands are also passing-through places, and the end points of empire are also forks in the road. If frontiers are spaces of narrative closure, then borderlands are places where stories take unpredictable turns and rarely end as expected.[13]

And it is in this spirit of the open horizon of borderlands as actual spaces and as points of theoretical departure that it is possible for border knowledges to migrate to other analytic realms. On a practical policy level, Juan Carlos Velasco and his research team propose an "open-border immigration policy" founded on the cosmopolitan ideal of hospitality and the recognition of *ius migrandi* or the right to migrate. Open borders or, an alternative, the redistribution of wealth among nations, is a social justice issue and means of remedying inequities and reducing global poverty. They embrace the idea that such a proposal is utopian but one that is nonetheless viable with a change in perception of what is possible:

> It is quite possible that the proposal as we have just outlined it, despite the internal coherence that it might have, could be labeled *utopian*. In today's world, a world still adjusted to the model of sovereign national countries, a world that is still Westphalian (as the principle of non-interference in internal affairs is still in effect and national borders still deserve maximum international protection), the free circulation of persons certainly presents itself as something for which the right circumstances for its effective recognition still do not exist. But it is also true that this particular utopia is in the same line of those that have made the world move: a utopia of a world without slaves, or the utopia of a world without a subordinate gender, to mention only two examples of social goals that in other times seemed completely unobtainable. The proposal formulated here is, instead, a micro-utopia, which does not try to be a perfect world, a paradise on Earth, but simply to show a way to avoid or at least mitigate the great and constant evils generated by the obsession with control in which most contemporary countries are trapped, a little utopia concentrated on the prevention of damages caused by that controlling desire.[14]

This open-border policy signals a shift in the way we conceive of borders and our relationship to other peoples and nations. For Walter Mignolo "border thinking" signals the emergence of a new logic, one that contests and supercedes the dialectics and typologies of inclusion and exclusion, exteriority and interiority, and subject and object of knowledge.[15] Border thinking marks an aporia, an abyss from which new meaning and new thought emerges. Nicole Sheren adapts this idea to analysis of borderlands art and performance in which the border is a performed space, not just a space of performance, and is thus a site of negotiation that cannot be reduced to its geographical location. She calls this the "border problematic" within performance:

> There exists a conflict at the heart of performance, one involving definitions of inside and outside, border and *frontera*, location and

dislocation. It is a problematic of site—both moving away from it and between spaces. I term this conflict, the inability to resolve the issue of distance and perspective, the *border problematic*.[16]

She explores the idea of a "portable border," a phrase that circulates among artists and critics, from Guillermo Gómez Peña to Claire F. Fox, to signal the mobility and portability of the border, an idea in line with much of the speculative fictions about the border. The border is a productive zone through which artists, writers and thinkers explore the constitution of national and local identity at a time of the purported diminishment of the importance of national boundaries in globalization.

The border zone is a speculative frontier of open possibility, of constant renewal and reconfiguring, and future plans—evident in the work of speculative cultural productions or imaginative city plans. The border lends insight into the proximate, the intimate, and the strange. It is a place that brings together seemingly incompatible—even opposing—ideas, peoples, forces, and things. And it is a place where a new story emerges, one that is surprising, full of possibility and unexpected turns. If we heed the creative pulse of the borderlands, we might, like the speculative fictions, art and design that take place in these spaces, forge new remedies and directions for imagining the future of the border and migrant labor that defines, enhances, passes through, and inhabits these liminal zones.

Notes

1. Reese Jones, *Border Walls: Security and the War on Terror in the United States, India, and Israel* (London: Zed Books, 2012), 7.
2. Todd Miller, "Follow the Money: The University of Arizona's Border War." *NACLA Report on the Americas* 45:1 (2012) 26.
3. "Why Do States Build Walls? Political Economy, Security, and Border Stability." *Journal of Conflict Resolution* 61:2 (2017) 239–270.
4. Cited in Sandro Mezzadora and Brett Neilson, *Border as Method, or the Multiplication of Labor* (Durham: Duke University Press, 2013), 3.
5. *Border as Method*, ix.
6. Ibid, xi.
7. Slavoj Žižek, *Violence: Six Sideways Reflections* (New York: Picador, 2008).
8. Cedric Robinson, *Black Marxism: The Making of the Black Radical Tradition* (Chapel Hill: University of North Carolina, 2000).
9. Alicia Schmidt-Camacho, "Ciudadana X: Gender Violence and the Denationalization of Women's Rights in Ciudad Juárez, Mexico." *The New Centennial Review* 5:1 (2005) 255–292.
10. Todd Miller, "Border Patrol Capitalism." *NACLA Report on the Americas* 48:2 (2016) 152–153.
11. Ibid, 154–155.

12. Victor Konrad and John Everitt, "Borders and 'Belongers': Transnational Identities, Border Security, and Cross-Border Socio-Economic Integration in the United States Borderlands with Canada and the British Virgin Islands." *Comparative American Studies* 9:4 (2011) 289.
13. Pekka Hämäläinen and Samuel Truett, "On Borderlands." *The Journal of American History* 98:2 (September 2011) 338.
14. Juan Carlos Velasco, "Open-Border Immigration Policy." *Migraciones Internacionales* 8:4 (2016) 66.
15. Walter D. Mignolo, *Local Histories/Global Designs: Coloniality, Subaltern Knowledges, and Border Thinking* (Princeton, NJ: Princeton University Press, 2000).
16. Nicole Sheren, *Portable Borders: Performance Art and Politics on the U.S. Frontera since 1984* (Austin: University of Texas Press, 2015), 2.

Works Cited

Carter, David and Paul Poast. "Why Do States Build Walls? Political Economy, Security, and Border Stability." *Journal of Conflict Resolution* 61:2 (2017) 239–270.

de Genova, Nicholas. *Racial Transformations: Latinos and Asians Remaking the United States*. Ed. Nicholas de Genova. Durham: Duke University Press, 2006.

Flores, William V. and Rita Benmayor. *Latino Cultural Citizenship: Claiming Identity, Space, and Rights*. Boston: Beacon, 1997.

Fojas, Camilla. *Border Bandits: Hollywood on the Southern Frontier*. Austin: University of Texas Press, 2008.

Ganz, Marshall. "Not the Cesar Chavez I Knew." *The Nation*, 1 April 2014, np.

Garza, Alicia. "Afterword to the 2016 Edition." In *Disposable Domestics: Immigrant Women Workers in the Global Economy*. Ed. Grace Chang. Chicago: Haymarket Books, 2016, 209–214.

Gómez Peña, Guillermo. *The New World Border: Prophesies, Poems, & Loqueras for the End of the Century*. San Francisco: City Lights, 1996.

Hämäläinen, Pekka and Samuel Truett. "On Borderlands." *The Journal of American History* 98:2 (September 2011) 338–361.

Ingle, Zachary. "The Border Crossed Us: *Machete* and the Latino Threat Narrative." In *Critical Approaches to the Films of Robert Rodriguez*. Ed. Frederick Aldama. Austin: University of Texas Press, 2014, 157–174.

Jones, Reese. *Border Walls: Security and the War on Terror in the United States, India, and Israel*. London: Zed Books, 2012.

Konrad, Victor and John Everitt. "Borders and 'Belongers': Transnational Identities, Border Security, and Cross-Border Socio-Economic Integration in the United States Borderlands with Canada and the British Virgin Islands." *Comparative American Studies* 9:4 (2011) 288–308.

Lilley, Sasha. *Capitalism and Its Discontents: Conversations With Radical Thinkers in a Time of Tumult*. Oakland: PM Press, 2011.

Maciel, David. *El Norte: The U.S-Mexican Border in Contemporary Cinema*. San Diego: Institution for the Regional Studies of the Californias, 1990.

Mann, Geoff. *Disassembly Required: A Field Guide to Actually Existing Capitalism*. Oakland: AK Press, 2013.

Marez, Curtiz. *Farm Worker Futurism: Speculative Technologies of Resistance*. Minneapolis: University of Minnesota Press, 2016.

Mata, Irene. *Domestic Disturbances: Reimagining Narratives of Gender, Labor, and Immigration*. Austin: University of Texas Press, 2014.

Mezzadora, Sandro and Brett Neilson. *Border as Method, or the Multiplication of Labor*. Durham and London: Duke University Press, 2013.

Mignolo, Walter D. *Local Histories/Global Designs: Coloniality, Subaltern Knowledges, and Border Thinking*. Princeton, NJ: Princeton University Press, 2000.

Miller, Todd. "Follow the Money: The University of Arizona's Border War." *NACLA Report on the Americas* 45:1 (2012) 23–26.

———. "Border Patrol Capitalism." *NACLA Report on the Americas* 48:2 (2016) 150–156.

Molina-Guzmán, Isabel. *Dangerous Curves: Latina Bodies in the Media*. New York: New York University Press, 2010.

Ontiveros, Randy. "No Golden Age: Television News and the Chicano Civil Rights Movement." In *The Race and Media Reader*. Ed. Gilbert B. Rodman. New York: Routledge, 2014.

Rivera, Lysa. "Future Histories and Cyborg Labor: Reading Borderlands Science Fiction after NAFTA." *Science Fiction Studies* 39:3 (2012) 415–436.

Robinson, Cedric. *Black Marxism: The Making of the Black Radical Tradition*. Chapel Hill: University of North Carolina Press, 2000.

Romero, Fernando. *Hyperborder: The Contemporary U.S.-Mexico Border and Its Future*. New York: Princeton Architectural Press, 2007.

Romero, Fernando et al. *Border City*. http://www.fr-ee.org/project/73/Border+City

Romero, Mary. *Maid in the U.S.A.* New York: Routledge, 1992.

Romero, Mary, Valerie Preston, and Wenona Giles. "Care Work in a Globalizing World." In *When Care Work Goes Global: Locating the Social Relations of Domestic Work*. Eds. Mary Romero, Valerie Preston, and Wenona Giles. Surrey: Ashgate, 2014, 1–28.

Sanchez, Rosaura and Beatrice Pita. *Lunar Braceros 2125–2149*. National City, Califas: Calaca Press, 2009.

Schmidt-Camacho, Alicia. "Ciudadana X: Gender Violence and the Denationalization of Women's Rights in Ciudad Juárez, Mexico." *The New Centennial Review* 5:1 (2005) 255–292.

Sheren, Nicole. *Portable Borders: Performance Art and Politics on the U.S. Frontera since 1984*. Austin: University of Texas Press, 2015.

Tobar, Hector. *The Barbarian Nurseries*. New York: Farrar, Strauss and Giroux, 2011.

Treviño, Jesús Salvador. *Eyewitness: A Filmmaker's Memoir of the Chicano Movement*. Houston: Arte Público Press, 2001.

Velasco, Juan Carlos. "Open-Border Immigration Policy." *Migraciones Internationacionales* 8:4 (2016) 41–72.

Wolff, Richard D. *Capitalism's Crisis Deepens: Essays on the Global Economic Meltdown 2010–2014*. Chicago: Haymarket Books, 2016.

Wright, Melissa W. "Public Women, Profit, and Femicide in Northern Mexico." *South Atlantic Quarterly* 105:4 (2006) 681–698.

Žižek, Slavoj. *Violence: Six Sideways Reflections*. New York: Picador, 2008.

Index